Decorative Woodwork

By the same author

Designs for Wood
Practical Woodwork
Modern Woodwork Book 1
Modern Woodwork Book 2
Step by Step in Woodworking

Christus Rex. Figure in lime 1000mm high, 615mm wide. Designed and carved by the author. Photograph Michael Solley.

Decorative Woodwork

Alonzo W. P. Kettless

Evans

Evans Brothers Limited

Published by Evans Brothers Limited,
Montague House, Russell Square,
London, W.C.1.

First published 1978
Reprinted 1980

Set in 10 on 11 point Univers
and printed in Great Britain by
Hazell Watson & Viney Limited,
Aylesbury, Bucks

ISBN 0 237 44845 9 PRA 6849

CONTENTS

Acknowledgements

The author and publishers would like to thank the following firms for kindly supplying photographs: Heal and Son Ltd., Gordon Russell Ltd., Record Ridgway Education Service, Emmerich (Berlon) Ltd., Stanley Works (GB) Ltd.

The author would like to thank Dr. Smith, Principal of Shoreditch College for permission to use photographs of work produced by students of Shoreditch College;

his colleague Jim Fowles, principal lecturer (Wood), Department of Design Technology;

his wife, Rose-Mary, for her unfailing support and for typing the manuscript;

his very special pupil, Alfred Gorvin, who started learning woodwork at the age of 77;

Joan Gubbin and the staff of Evans Brothers Limited for their enthusiasm and co-operation in the production of this book;

Laurence Gall of Lowestoft for his skill and patience in taking many of the photographs.

The line drawings are the work of the author or have been reproduced from the author's originals by Ken Harvey of Illustrated Arts. The various carvings, sculptures and models not credited were all designed and made by the author.

INTRODUCTION

The main aim of this book is to encourage a fresh and lively approach to the art of decorative woodwork using one of the most versatile of all natural materials. It is also hoped that it will provide an extensive source of information for beginners and craftsmen alike and be of guidance in the development of artistic appreciation in the field of craft work.

An attempt has been made to promote good design and craftsmanship. A wide range of craft techniques and experimental work is introduced, with emphasis placed on the use of hand tools in producing an individual piece of work—a process which is both satisfying and therapeutic.

Alonzo W. P. Kettless,
Suffolk, 1977

TIMBER AND MANUFACTURED BOARD

Wood is one of the world's most useful and versatile materials. Obtainable in a variety of sizes, colours and textures, it can be worked with edge tools—saws, planes and chisels—and is used extensively in the building and furniture industries. Even the waste is utilized in the production of hardboard, chipboard and other man-made materials.

Trees have a complex cellular structure and are divided into two main categories: hardwood or broad-leaf trees, and softwood or needle-leaved trees. The latter are usually cone bearing and are often referred to as conifers.

Fig. 1 shows a section through a tree. The main parts are: growth rings—these consist of springwood which is the light inner part of the ring and summerwood which is the denser portion of the ring; sapwood which is the outer portion of the tree, usually light in colour, softer than and of inferior quality to the heartwood; rays which are storage tissue and convey food to all parts of the tree; heartwood, usually the dark inner portion of the tree, producing the most durable timber for commercial purposes and bark which surrounds the tree and forms a protective covering especially for new growth.

Conversion

The cell and cell walls of newly felled trees contain a large proportion of water, the sapwood containing more moisture than the heartwood. After the tree is felled it is necessary to break down the log (to saw it into smaller sections) as soon as possible. This process is called conversion. Early conversion reduces the risk of splitting as shown in Fig. 2. Wood shrinks as the moisture dries out of it and splits are caused by uneven and too rapid drying.

The drawings are mainly self explanatory. Fig. 3 shows the effect of shrinkage on a log which has been quartered. Note the change of shape in relation to the squares before and after seasoning. Fig. 3A illustrates and compares the amount of shrinkage likely between flat- and quarter-sawn timber. A common method of converting softwood logs is shown in Fig. 4 while Fig. 5 shows a typical hardwood log and method of conversion to remove heart defects. Fig. 6 shows a method of quartering a log to give a large proportion of stable and figured material and Fig. 7 gives a method used in the timber trade to produce true wainscot oak of good quality and figure. Note the crown or heart plank and method of removing heart defect.

The most economical cut is the through-and-through flat or slash-sawn method, shown in Fig. 8. The quarter-sawn method produces timber which is more stable and in some instances, particularly oak, better figured. The extra work involved in converting a quarter-sawn log makes it more expensive than plain sawn timber.

Seasoning

Before freshly cut or green timber can be used for constructional purposes it must be carefully seasoned to meet the requirements of the consumer.

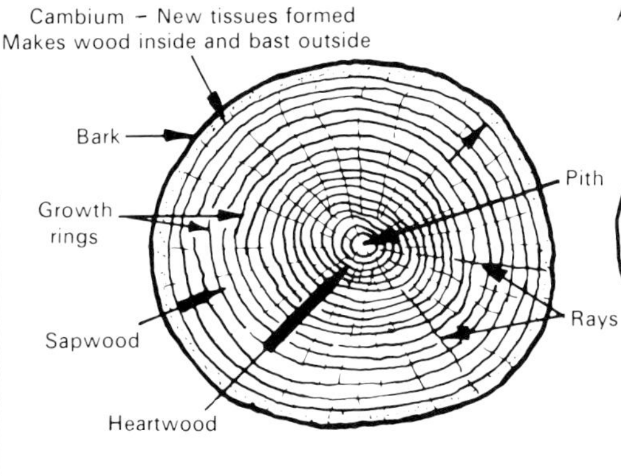

Section through tree

Fig. 1

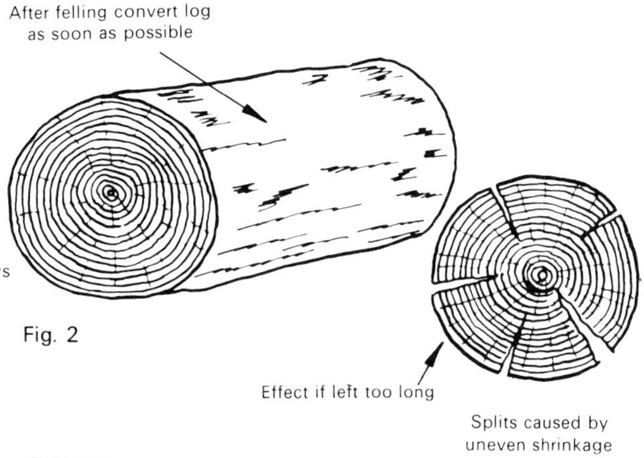

Fig. 2

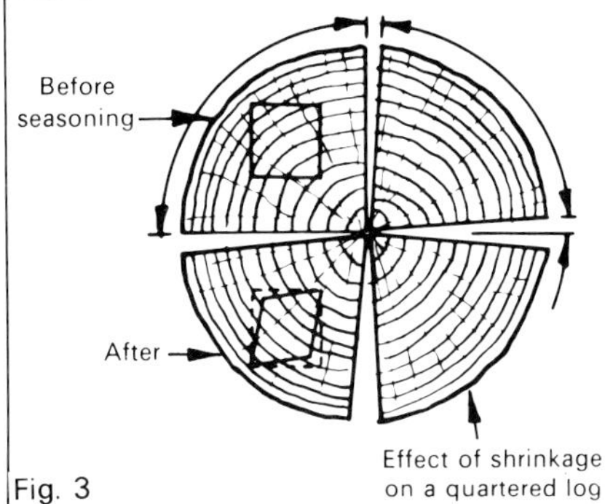

Fig. 3

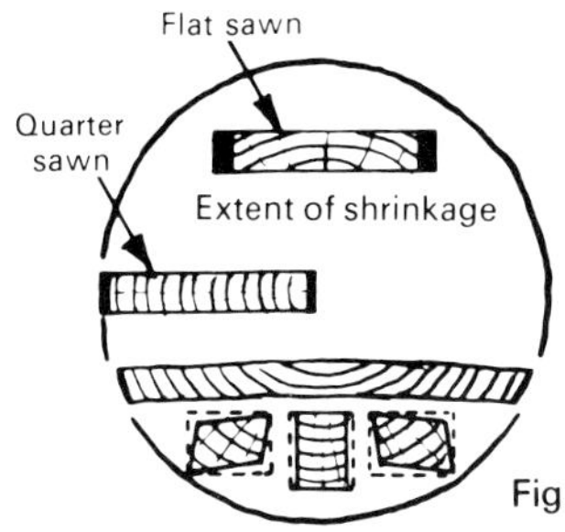

Fig. 3A

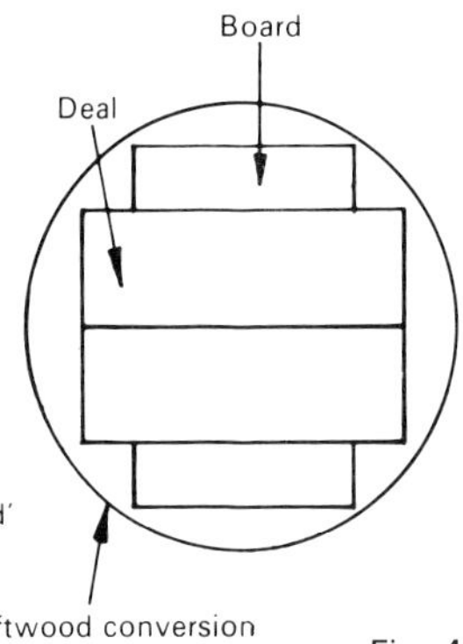

Fig. 4

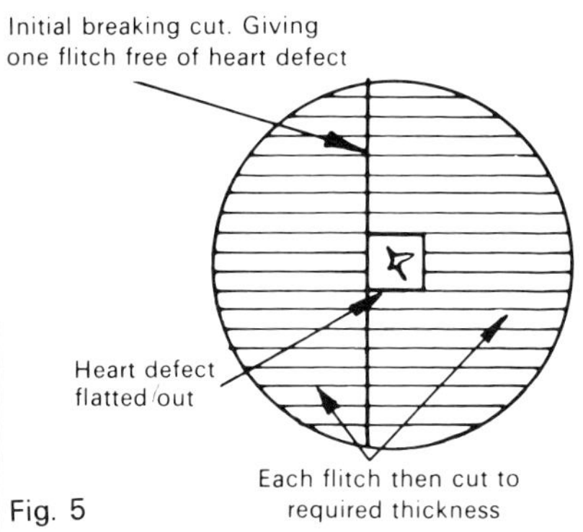

Fig. 5

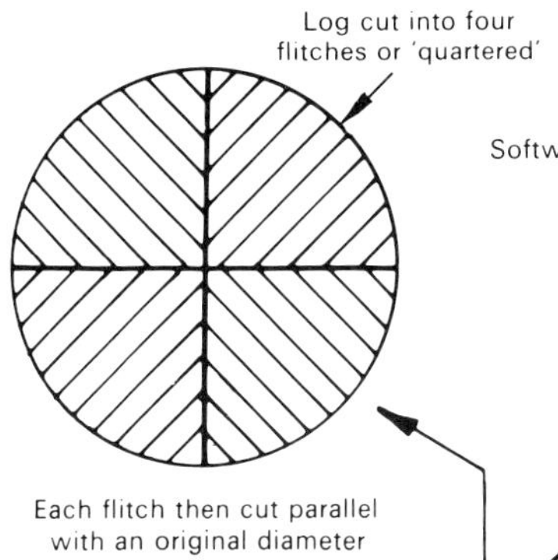

Fig. 6 Method of quartering a log

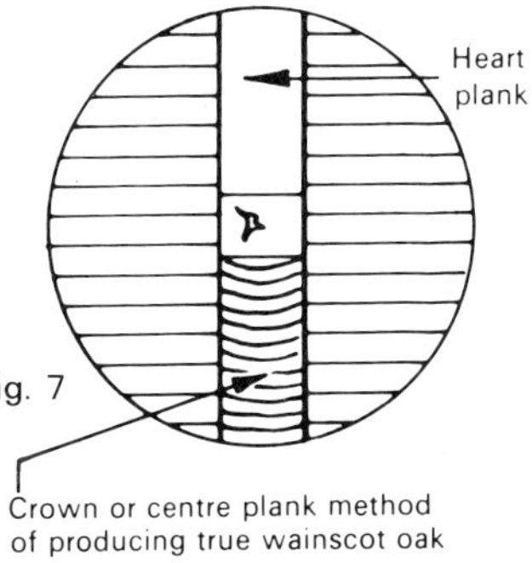

Fig. 7

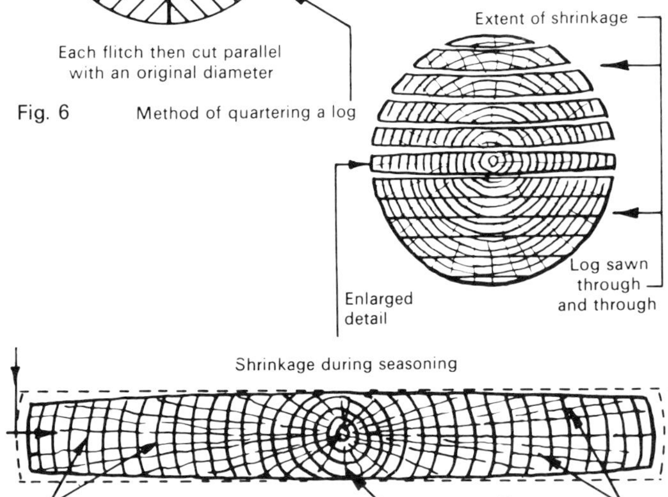

Fig. 8

Natural or air seasoning

Most timber yards have a good variety of logs stacked in open sheds for seasoning, the roof keeping off rain and effects of the sun.

Fig. 9 shows the timber properly stacked for air seasoning. Note the method of stacking and the arrangement of the piling sticks, spaced at intervals from 500mm.-1000mm. ($19\frac{3}{4}$in.-$39\frac{1}{2}$in.) according to thickness of material. The sticks, which must be placed vertically one above the other, allow the air to circulate freely around the planks or boards. Note that the stack must be kept well clear of the floor.

Air seasoning is a slow process taking approximately one year for every 25mm. (1in.) of thickness and it leaves the wood with a moisture content of about 18 per cent.

Kiln seasoning

Kiln seasoning is an artificial and rapid method of seasoning by which means timber can be conditioned to suit any particular requirement.

Even after seasoning, wood is always on the move, shrinking and expanding in width, according to changes in humidity. This movement must be allowed for in construction. Wood is strongest in its length, and shrinkage in that direction is for all practical purposes negligible.

Defects

These in timber are many and varied, some are caused naturally such as knots and internal shakes, others are caused by careless felling, converting and stacking. Some defects such as sound knots, if well placed and decorative, can often enhance the work.

Defects to be avoided

Knots: Generally to be avoided in constructional work such as chair legs, or any situation where they would weaken the member. Knots, if sound and well placed, could be decorative such as in knotty pine panelling.
End splits: The separation or rupture of the wood tissue, extending to both sides of the board, see Fig. 10A.
Checks: Surface rupture only, Fig. 10B.

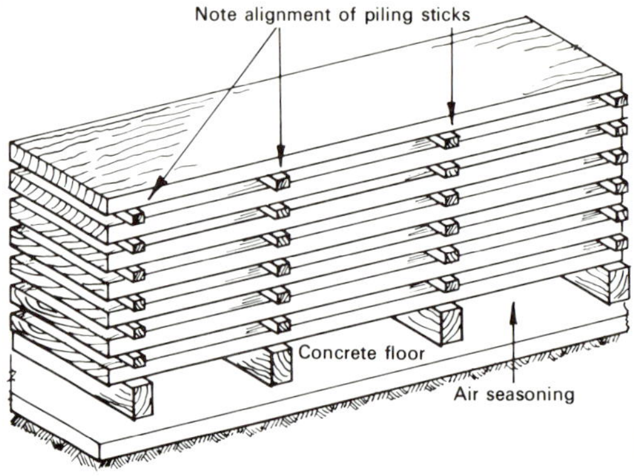

Fig. 9

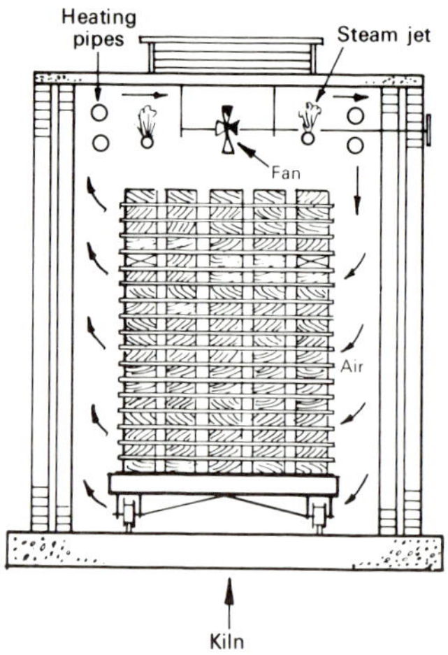

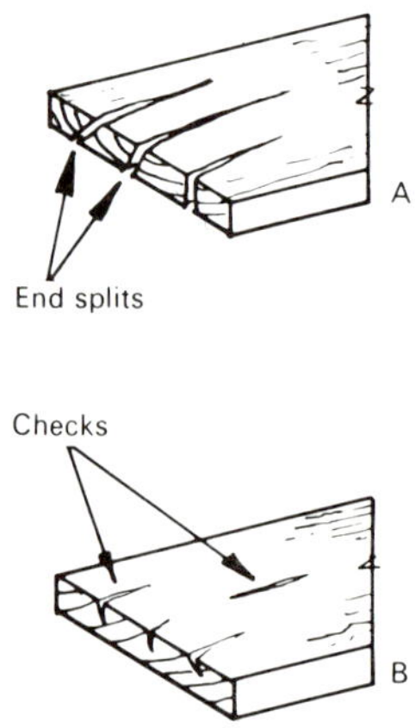

Fig. 10

Twisting: The spiral warping of a board or plank in a longitudinal direction, see Fig. 10C.
Cupping: This is warping across the width of the board, it does not occur in quarter sawn timber, see Fig. 10D.
Bowing: The warping or sagging from end to end of a board or plank is called bowing. This is often caused by careless stacking e.g. when the piling sticks are placed too far apart, see Fig. 10E.
Note: twisting, bowing and cupping are mainly the unchecked effect of shrinkage; good stacking before drying commences will do much to prevent this kind of defect.
Heart shake: A natural defect which is more common in trees past their prime, Fig. 10F.
Ring shake: This is where the separation follows a growth ring. It is usually an injury caused by insects, drought, or frost during growth, see Fig. 10G.
Sapwood: The outer portion of a tree, usually of inferior quality to the heartwood. It is liable to be attacked by wood boring beetles.

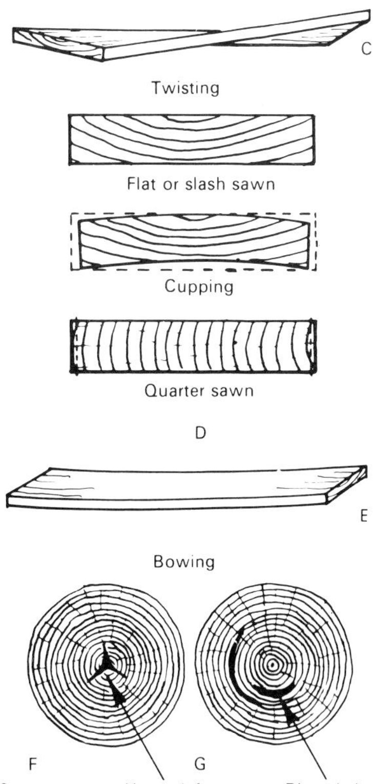

Fig. 10

Buying and selecting timber

The above summary deals with some of the many defects to be avoided when selecting and purchasing timber. Get to know your local and country timber merchants. Some stock only softwoods, while others will deal mainly in home-grown or foreign hardwoods. Very often good, sound pieces of hardwood suitable for carving can be found lying around the timber yards.

Wood that is imported into Britain is usually in the sawn state, as cut or converted by the mill which prepared it for export. This material can be purchased in the sawn sizes. If you require your material to be planed all round, simply specify P.A.R. This means that the sawn material has been planed all round and the planing will have made it approximately 3mm. ($\frac{1}{8}$in.) smaller in both width and thickness. Not all hardwood merchants are equipped with planing machines, so you must be prepared to plane your purchased material or make arrangements with a local joiners shop to do this for you.

Useful pieces of timber for carving can also be obtained when friends are pruning or felling small trees. The best time for cutting down timber is between November and early March when the sap is at rest. Laburnum, yew, cherry, pear, apple, walnut, holly and box are particularly suitable for carving and the author has been collecting such woods for many years. Any small pieces of tree should be stored carefully in dry, well ventilated conditions and allowed to dry slowly away from sunlight and heat. Sealing the end grain with paint or hot, melted paraffin wax helps to prevent splitting.

A small piece of laburnum or yew, approximately 50mm. (2in.) in diameter to be used for oyster shell work or carving, could take up to three years to dry out. So you will appreciate it is never too soon to start building up your stocks.

Manufactured boards

Plywood: One of the best known boards, plywood, consists of an odd number of veneers in sheet form, laid and glued together so that the grain of each piece is at

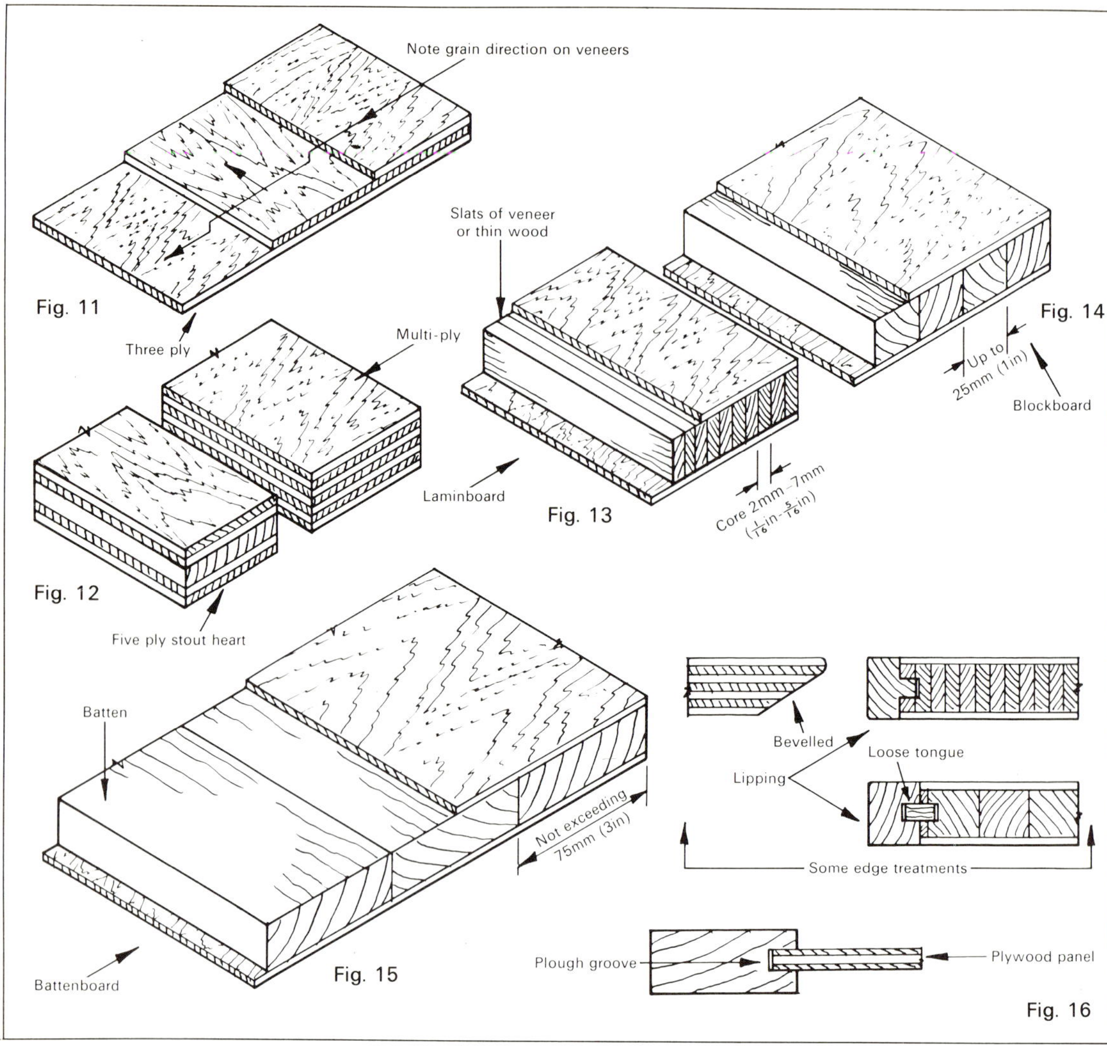

right angles to that of the next, see Fig. 11. This arrangement of veneers or plies gives plywood its special qualities, such as stability, strength and flexibility as opposed to shrinkage or warping in solid timber. A good selection of sizes is usually available, with thicknesses ranging from approximately $1\frac{1}{2}$mm.-12mm. ($\frac{1}{16}$in.-$\frac{1}{2}$in.).

Multi-ply: This is the term used for plywood of five or more plies, see Fig. 12. The author has designed and made several pieces of sculpture out of multi-plywood. This material offers great possibilities for creative sculpture and simple forms of carving. Note how the alternate veneers and glue lines enhance the work, adding a distinctive character to the sculpture.

Laminboard: A very stable material, laminboard is suitable for high-class furniture. It is one of the more expensive boards with a core made up of slats of veneer or thin wood not exceeding 7mm. ($\frac{5}{16}$in.) in thickness and faced on both sides with one or more veneers, see Fig. 13.

Blockboard: Similar to laminboard. Blockboard has a core made up of blocks not exceeding 25mm. (1in.), Fig. 14. It is very good for such items as table tops and doors, but not so stable as laminboard.

Battenboard: The construction is similar to blockboard, but with a core consisting of battens not more than 75mm. (3in.) wide. All the above boards are obtainable in a good variety of sizes, see Fig. 15.

Hardboard: This consists of wood fibre formed into a cohesive slab which is subjected to great pressure at very high temperature, producing a tough and durable board. A wide variety of hardboard is available, including perforated hardboard or pegboard, hardboard surfaced with melamine, plastic-faced, veneered, moulded, embossed, or painted.

This versatile material is now employed in large quantities in industry and by home craftsmen. It is used for such purposes as panelling, flush doors, floor covering, table tops, trays, cut-out lettering, relief carvings, and display work. Hardboard is easily worked with ordinary hand tools and a fine-toothed saw should be used when cutting to size. It is obtainable in a wide range of large sheets, varying in thicknesses from 3mm. to 18mm. ($\frac{1}{8}$in. to $\frac{3}{4}$in.)

Wood chipboard: A constructional board consisting of softwood chips finely milled to a uniform size and bonded with Urea-formaldehyde synthetic resin. Chipboard can be purchased veneered on both sides. It is used in considerable quantities by the furniture industry and is suitable for such items as carcases and flush doors, flooring, (for which there exists a special dense grade) and partitioning. Available in a good selection of sizes, its thickness usually ranges from 12mm. to 18mm. ($\frac{1}{2}$in. to $\frac{3}{4}$in.) and over.

Edge treatments: Lipping is used to finish the edges of multi-ply, laminboard, block-board and the like. A variety of edge treatments suitable for table tops, doors and plaques are shown in Fig. 16.

Timbers for woodworking

There are hundreds of species of tree and a large proportion are suitable for woodworking. Those experienced in working in wood will have used a number of these timbers and through the years developed an appreciation and an understanding of the varied and sometimes intricate character of wood. They know the meaning of such terms as 'straight' and 'interlocking grain,' 'of even texture'; study the sole of a wooden jack plane and you will notice the close, firm, smooth and compact nature of beech. A knowledge would also be required of the various weights, colour, aroma, strength, and tactile qualities of timber and of the fact that some woods split more easily than others.

The following list of timbers are given simply as a guide. The author recommends that students and beginners start a collection of specimen pieces of wood and actually saw, plane, chisel, gouge, scrape and experiment with a variety of finishes, making notes and comparing the qualities of the different species. A sound knowledge of timber can only be developed from actually working and cutting the material.

HOME GROWN HARDWOODS

Species and approx. weights per cu.ft.	Colour, texture, figure, etc.	Firmness and workability, uses, etc.
Apple (Malus pumila and pyrus malus) 48lbs.	Pink. Fine even texture.	Tough, cuts cleanly. Ideal for mallets, turnery and small pieces of carving. Stable.
Ash (Fraxinus excelsior) 46lbs.	White, pinky-cream to light brown. Coarse texture. Plain-to-decorative features.	Works well. A tough flexible timber, ideal for steam bending and laminating. Stable.
Beech (Fagus sylvatica) approx. 44lbs.	Whitish-yellow. Fine close and even texture. Some decorative features according to method of conversion.	Medium hard. Suitable for turnery and carving. Excellent for steam bending and laminated work. Stable.
Box (Buxus sempervirens) approx. 65lbs.	Creamy-yellow. Very close even texture.	Hard. Suitable for work of fine detail. Excellent for turnery and inlay work. The timber is only available in small sections, and is usually sold by weight.
Cherry (Prunus avium) 39lbs.	Pinkish-brown. Fine even texture.	Medium hard. Clean working. Takes a fine finish. Excellent for pattern making. Stable.

Species and approx. weights per cu.ft.	Colour, texture, figure, etc.	Firmness and workability, uses, etc.
Chestnut, sweet (Castanea sativa) 28lbs.	Pale golden brown. Resembles oak in appearance, but has no visible silver ray.	Softer than English oak. Carves and turns well. Stable.
Elm (Ulmus procera) 36lbs.	Pale to medium brown. Coarse texture. Bold decorative figure.	Hard, tough and durable. Works cleanly. Takes a good finish. Bends well when straight grained. Care needed when seasoning.
Holly (Ilex aquifolium) approx. 47lbs.	White to greyish-white. Dense even texture.	Hard. Very clean working. Takes a fine finish. Suitable for small carvings and inlay work. Stains well.
Laburnum (Laburnum anagyroides) approx. 50lbs.	Rich olive brown. Even texture. Growth rings produce striking figure.	Medium hard. Ideal for small figure carving. Very decorative when cut to produce 'oysters' for inlay work.
Lime (Tilia vulgaris) 37lbs.	Yellowish-white. Fine uniform texture. Little figure.	Carves beautifully. Firm and crisp with reasonable hardness. Fairly stable when seasoned.
Oak (Quercus robur) 49lbs.	Golden yellow, darkens with age. Coarse even texture. Quarter-sawn oak produces very attractive figure.	Medium hard to hard. Carves well. Very durable. Excellent for architectural work and furniture making. Straight grained material bends well.

Species and approx. weights per cu.ft.	Colour, texture, figure, etc.	Firmness and workability, uses, etc.
Pear (Pyrus communis) 47lbs.	Pinkish-brown. Has a very fine even texture.	Medium hard. Works well. Very stable. Ideal for figure carving and turning.
Sycamore (Acer pseudoplatanus) 38lbs.	Milk-white colour, inclined to darken to yellowish brown on exposure. Close even texture.	Medium hard to hard. Fine silky finish. Carves and turns well.
Walnut (Juglans regia) 43lbs.	Greyish light brown to rich brown. The best timber is usually finely figured. Even texture.	Medium hard. Excellent for carving and furniture making. Takes polish well. Stable.

SOME FOREIGN HARDWOODS

Species and approx. weights per cu.ft.	Colour, texture, figure, etc.	Firmness and workability, uses, etc.
Blackbean (Castanospermum australe) 46lbs.	Chocolate brown. Straight grained, even texture.	Hard. Works cleanly. Capable of a fine finish. Stable.
Lignum vitae West Indies etc. (Guaiacum officinale) 80lbs.	Dark green, with brown streaks. Fine close grain.	Very hard and heavy. Has a slight greasy nature. Will carve and turn well. Stable.
Mahogany, African (Khaya ivorenis etc.) 33lbs.	Light pink brown to reddish-brown. Fairly coarse texture. Stripy figure.	Medium hard. Some interlocking grain. Works well with sharp tools. Fairly stable.
Mahogany, Honduras (Swietenia macrophylla) 36lbs.	Reddish-brown. Close even texture. Figure—varies from rich to plain lustrous figure.	Medium hard. Carves well. Generally very good working properties. Very stable.
Muninga, African (Pterocarpus angolensis) 40lbs.	Golden brown. Richly streaked. Coarse to medium fine texture.	Medium hard. Clean working. Takes polish well. Stable.

Species and approx. weights per cu.ft.	Colour, texture, figure, etc.	Firmness and workability, uses, etc.
Rosewood, Rio (Dalbergia various)	Blackish or purple brown, with stripy markings. Medium coarse texture.	Hard. Works well but tools need frequent sharpening. Stable.
Rosewood, Bombay 57lbs.	Dark brown-purple-black. Fairly straight grain. Medium coarse oily texture.	Harder than Rio. Works well and capable of a fine finish. Stable.
Teak, India, Burma (Tectona grandis) 45lbs.	Light to dark golden-brown, with occasional dark streaks. Coarse even texture.	Medium hard. Carves well but tends to blunt tools. An excellent all-round timber. Stable.
Utile, African Sapele. (Entandrophragma sp.)	Greyish-pink to red. Quarter sawn produces a pleasant stripe.	Moderately hard. Clean working. Can be obtained in fairly large sizes. A good all-round timber. Tends to be unstable unless quarter-sawn.
Walnut, African (Lovoa klaineana) 31lbs.	Bronzy-yellow. Lustrous with dark streaks. Coarse even texture with ribbon stripes.	Medium hard. Easy to work, but interlocking grain. can be troublesome. Used for high class joinery and furniture. Fairly stable.
Walnut, American (Juglans nigra) 37lbs.	Rich purple brown. Fine even texture. Attractive figure. Medium coarse texture.	Moderately hard. Clean working. Takes a good finish. Excellent for carving and furniture. Stable.

SOFTWOODS

Species and approx. weights per cu.ft.	Colour, texture, figure, etc.	Firmness and workability, uses, etc.
Douglas fir (Pseudotsuga taxifolia) 33lbs.	Light reddish brown. An attractive straight grained timber. Texture variable.	Moderately easy to work. Carves well. Used extensively in the building industries, and for the manufacture of plywood. Stable.
Pine (Pinus sylvestris) Alternatively known as: Scots pine Red Baltic pine Red pine Redwood 26lbs.	Colour varies from yellow to reddish brown. Growth rings are clearly marked by the contrasting light springwood and the darker summerwood zones.	Moderately strong. Easy to work. Takes paint and stain readily. Used extensively in the building industry.
Yellow pine (Pinus strobus) 26lbs.	Pale yellowish white. Even texture.	Easy to work. Excellent for carving and pattern making. Generally scarce. Very stable.
Yew (Taxus baccata) 49lbs.	Attractive golden brown markings. Fine close even texture. Subject to knots, shakes, etc. A delightful material.	Hard durable timber. Works well. Excellent for turnery and carving.

TOOLS AND EQUIPMENT

This section has been planned to introduce some of the principal tools used in woodworking so as to enable the beginner to select and build up a tool kit with some degree of confidence.

When purchasing tools it is economical to buy only the best and those which bear the name of a reputable manufacturer. Good tools are an investment.

Saws

Saws used by the woodworker can be divided into two categories, those used for ripping, that is cutting *along* the grain, and those for cross-cutting, that is sawing *across* the grain.

Rip saw: Recommended size, length 660mm. (26in.), 4 points to every 25mm. (1in.). It is economical to use a portable power saw where a large quantity of timber has to be ripped to size. Fig. 1 shows the outline of the teeth, with an end view of the saw blade showing 'set'.
Cross-cut or hand-saw: This is a very popular and useful saw, Fig. 2. Recommended size 660mm. (26in.), 8 points to every 25mm. (1in.). The teeth on the cross-cut saw are sharpened at an angle which produces needle-like points, enabling the saw to cut cleanly across the grain. These saws can also be used for cutting thin material along the grain. Fig. 3 shows the outline of the teeth of a cross-cut saw.
Panel saw: Recommended size, length 560mm. (22in.), 11 points to every 25mm. (1in.). Smaller than the hand-saw, it is used for fine work, such as cross-cutting thin panels, plywood, laminboard and for ripping thin material along the grain.
Tenon saw: Recommended size, length 305mm. (12in.), 14 points to every 25mm. (1in.). The saw in Fig. 4 is most useful for general purposes, as well as for cutting tenons and dovetails. It is sometimes called a back saw, because it has a back of brass or steel to stiffen the blade.
Dovetail saw: A smaller version of the tenon saw, it has finer teeth and very little 'set'. Used for fine dovetailing and similar work. Recommended size 203mm. (8in.), 20 points to every 25mm. (1in.).
Coping saw: Blade length, 152mm. (6in.). This saw, Fig. 5, is used for cutting fine curves, removing waste in dovetailing, and for the scribing of mouldings.
Fret saw: A fret saw, Fig. 6, is particularly useful for cutting shapes in plywood and for wood jewellery. Different grades and types of blades are obtainable. Frame size 355mm. (14in.).
Keyhole or pad saw: This saw, Fig. 7, is used for small work particularly where there is limited space to operate, or where a larger saw would be an obstruction. Blade length 305mm. (12in.).

Planes

Planes are important tools used by the woodworker to work and shape wood to given sizes and to prepare surfaces for different finishes.

Wood Jack plane: Made of selected beech, a wood Jack plane is still used by the craftsman. It certainly needs expert attention to maintain it in good working

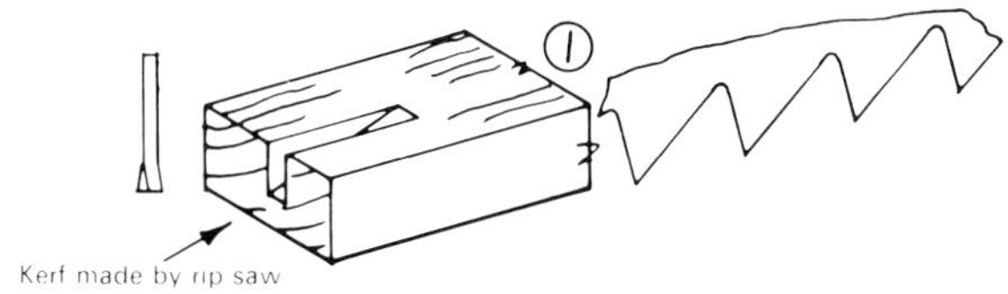

Fig. 1

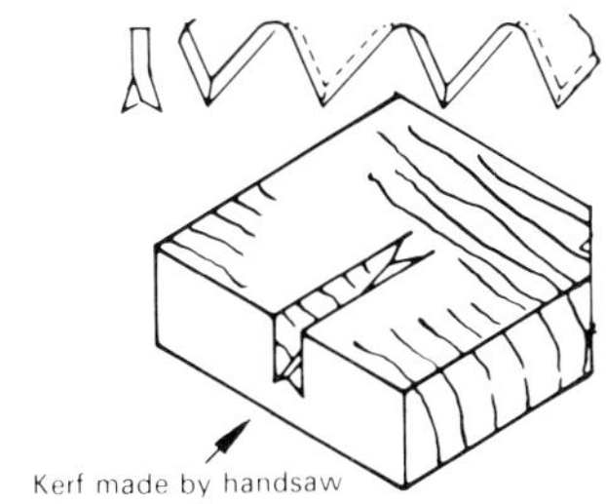

Fig. 3

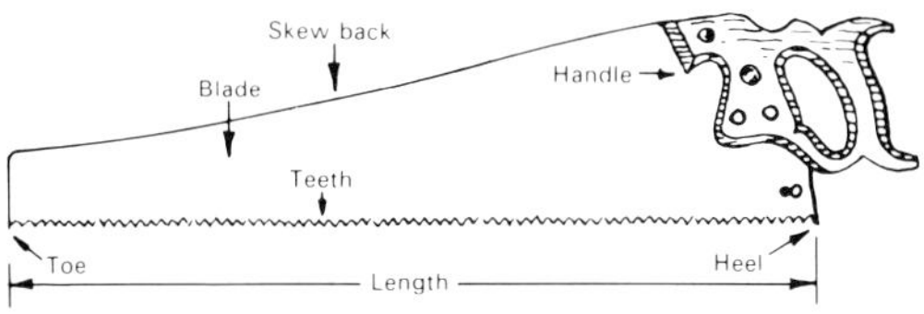

Fig. 2

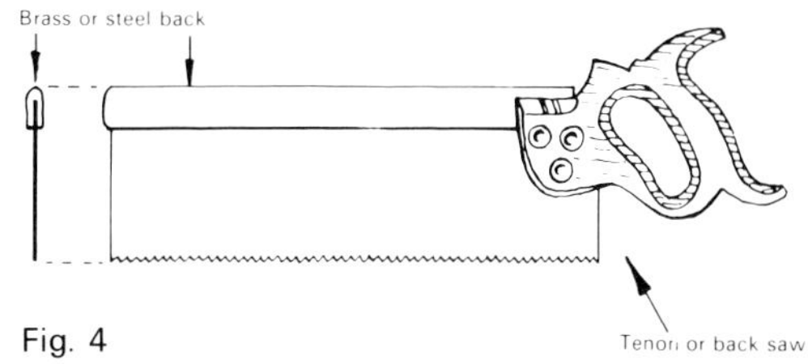

Fig. 4

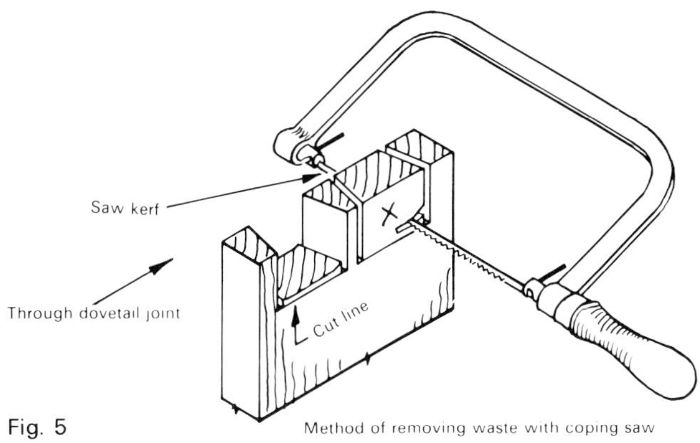

Fig. 5

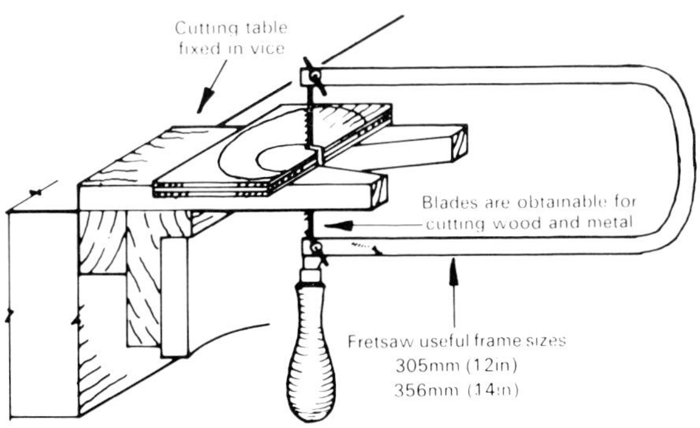

Fig. 6

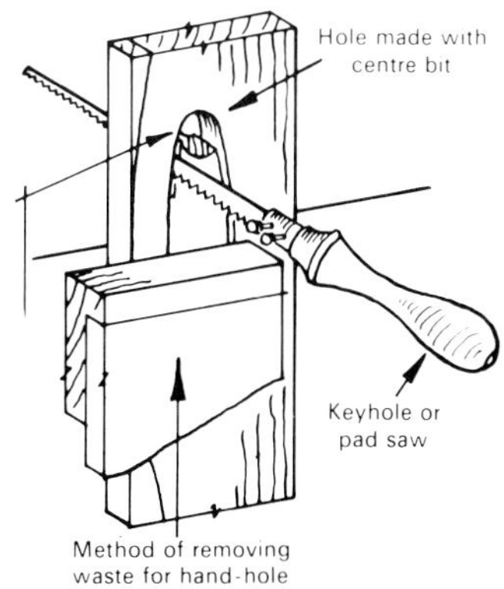

Fig. 7

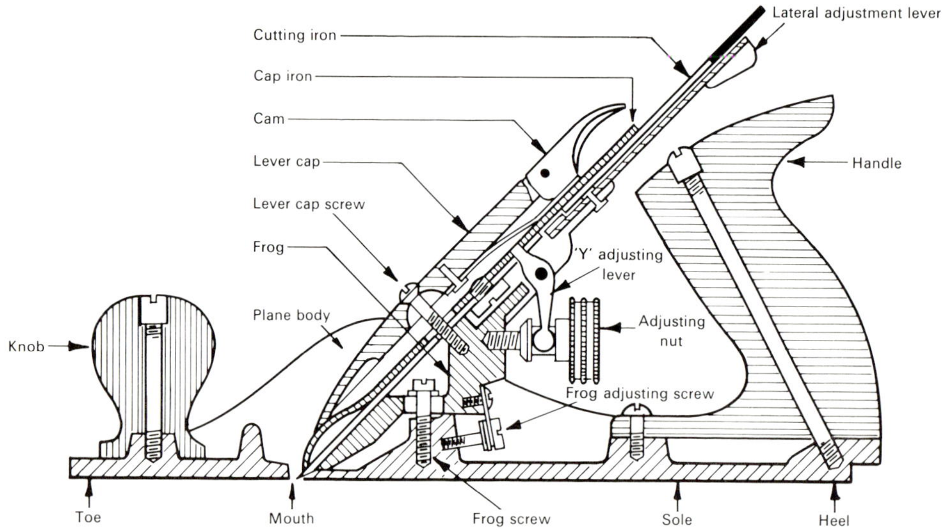

Fig. 8

condition. A useful size is 405mm. (16in.) with a 57mm. ($2\frac{1}{4}$in.) cutter.

Metal Jack plane: Recommended size 380mm. (15in.) long, with a 60mm. ($2\frac{3}{8}$in.) cutter. The modern metal planes are reliable and easily adjusted and will remain flat and true. Fig. 8 shows the sectional elevation of a metal plane. Fig. 9 shows a Jack plane.

Trying plane: Recommended size 560mm. (22in.) long, with a 60mm. ($2\frac{3}{8}$in.) cutter. Longer than the Jack plane. Now mainly manufactured in metal, although wood trying planes are still obtainable. They are used for making large surfaces flat and for 'shooting' joints, the truing up of material for edge jointing.

Smoothing plane: Recommended size 230mm. (9in.) long with 50mm. (2in.) cutter. A smoothing plane is necessary for cleaning up, preparing surfaces for polishing or painting and general bench work.

Block plane: Smaller than the smoothing plane. A very versatile plane. Owing to its size and shape, a block plane can be held comfortably in one hand. It has a low-angled iron and is particularly useful for small work and the cleaning up of end grain. See Fig. 10.

Rebate plane: A very useful and versatile plane. A rebate plane is shown in Fig. 11, and typical examples of the work it can do are shown in Fig. 12.

Router: Essential when finishing housings or grooves to depth. See Fig. 13. The small router, Fig. 14, is particularly useful when inlaying.

Shoulder plane: A shoulder plane has a low-pitched (angled) cutting iron, which makes it particularly suitable for trimming shoulders and cleaning up rebates, see Fig. 15. This plane is essential for accurate work in hardwood.

Bull-nose plane: A very useful plane for cleaning up stopped rebates, mouldings. See Fig. 16.

Plough plane: This plane, illustrated in Fig. 17, is for making grooves, particularly for panels.

Spokeshave: A type of plane used for shaping and finishing work after using the bow or coping saw. It is also used for shaped work in carving, sculpture and mouldings and is available with a flat or round sole (bottom). See Fig. 18.

Rasps and files for wood: These are essential shaping tools used by craftsmen when edge tools cannot be employed efficiently. A 203mm. (8in.) half round medium

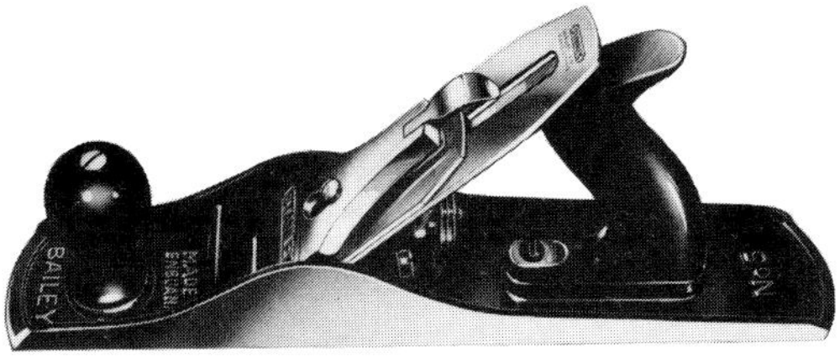

Fig. 9

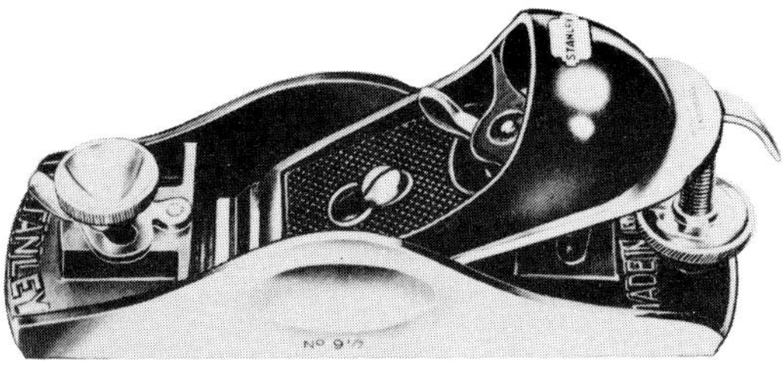

Fig. 10

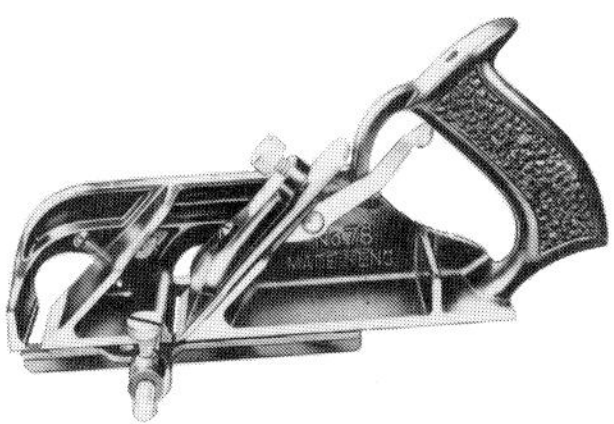

Fig. 11

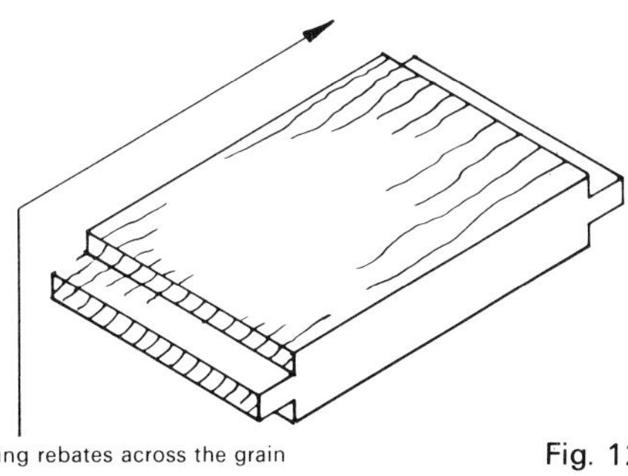

Fig. 12

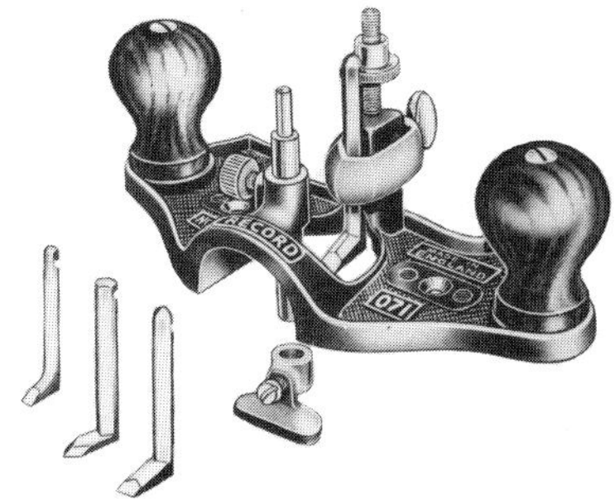

Fig. 13

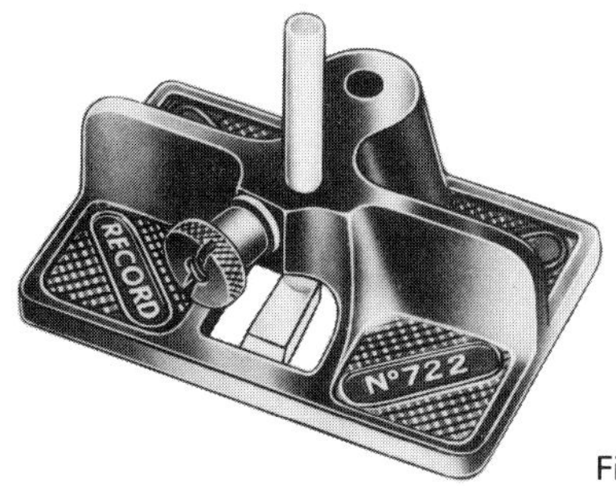

Fig. 14

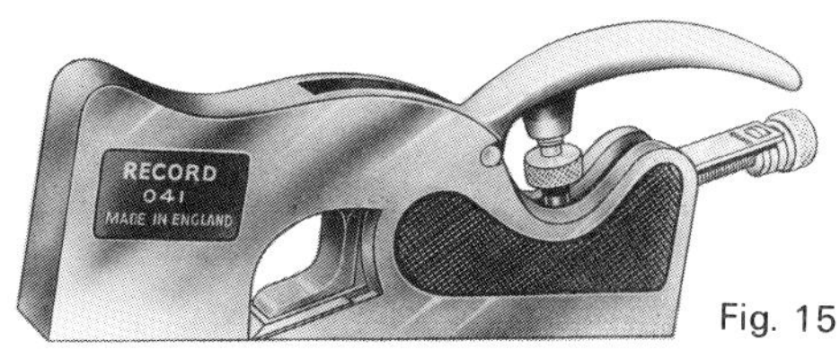

Fig. 15

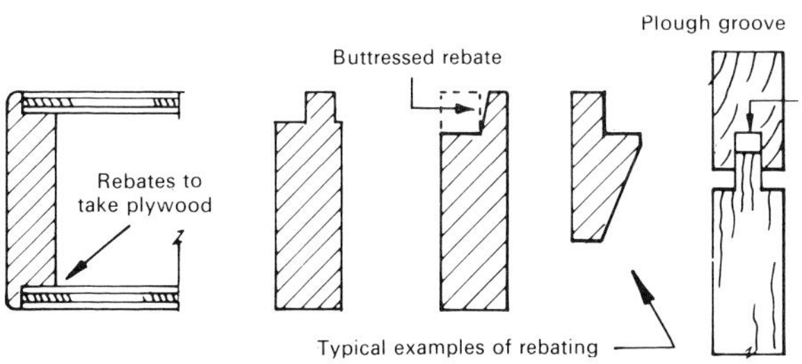

Fig. 9 Stanley No. 5 Jack plane.

Fig. 10 Block plane.

Fig. 11 Rebate plane with adjustable fence and depth gauge.

Fig. 13 Record router plane.

Fig. 14 Small router useful for model making

Fig. 15 Shoulder plane.

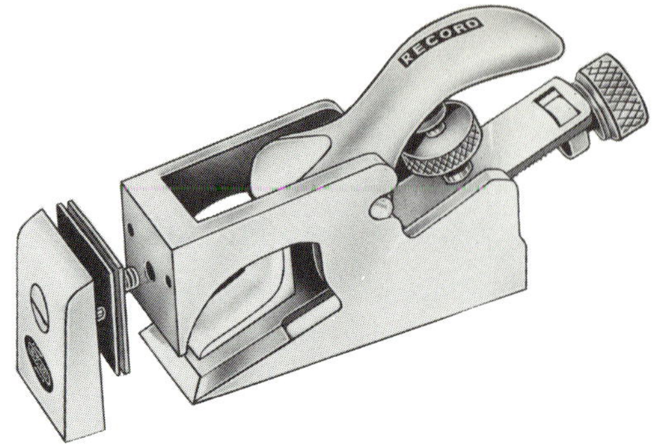

Fig. 16 (Above right) Improved bull-nose plane.
Fig. 17 (Left) Stanley three-blade plough plane.
Fig. 18 (Below) Flat and convex spokeshaves.

rasp and a 203mm. (8in.) medium wood file, are useful sizes. The Stanley range of Surform rasps and files are also useful, these are used for shaping hand holes for trays, shaped dishes, mouldings, plywood shaping, carving and sculpture. See Fig. 19.
Rifflers: Small shaped files are ideal for

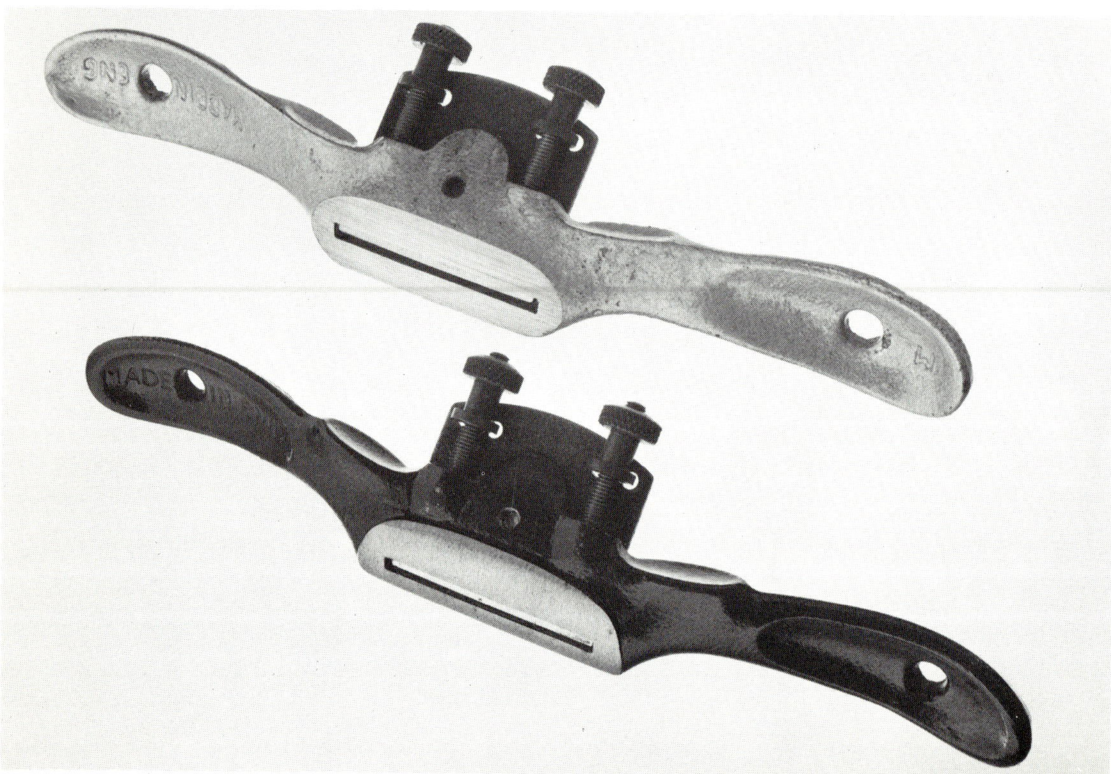

small and intricate detail work. They are made in many shapes and sizes.

Marking out and testing tools

Steel rule: A steel rule, 305mm. (12in.) is essential for measuring and testing.
Wood rule: A metre, four-fold boxwood rule is useful for general purposes.
Steel tape: Metric, callibrated in metric measurements. See Fig. 20.
Dividers: For spacing equal measurements.
Trammel heads: For fixing on wood bar; used for marking out large circles.
Winding strips: Essential for testing material and jobs for wind. A useful size for winding strips is 355mm. (14in.). These are usually made by the craftsman. See page 36.
Try square: Illustrated in Fig. 21, a try square is for testing the squareness of material

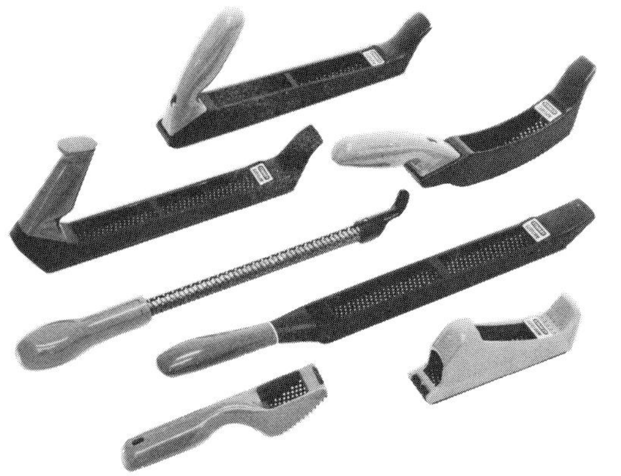

Fig. 19 (Top left) Stanley Surform tools.

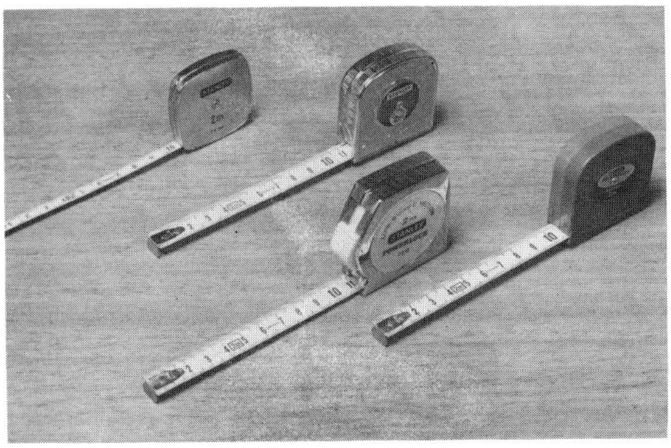

Fig. 20 (Centre left) Steel tapes.

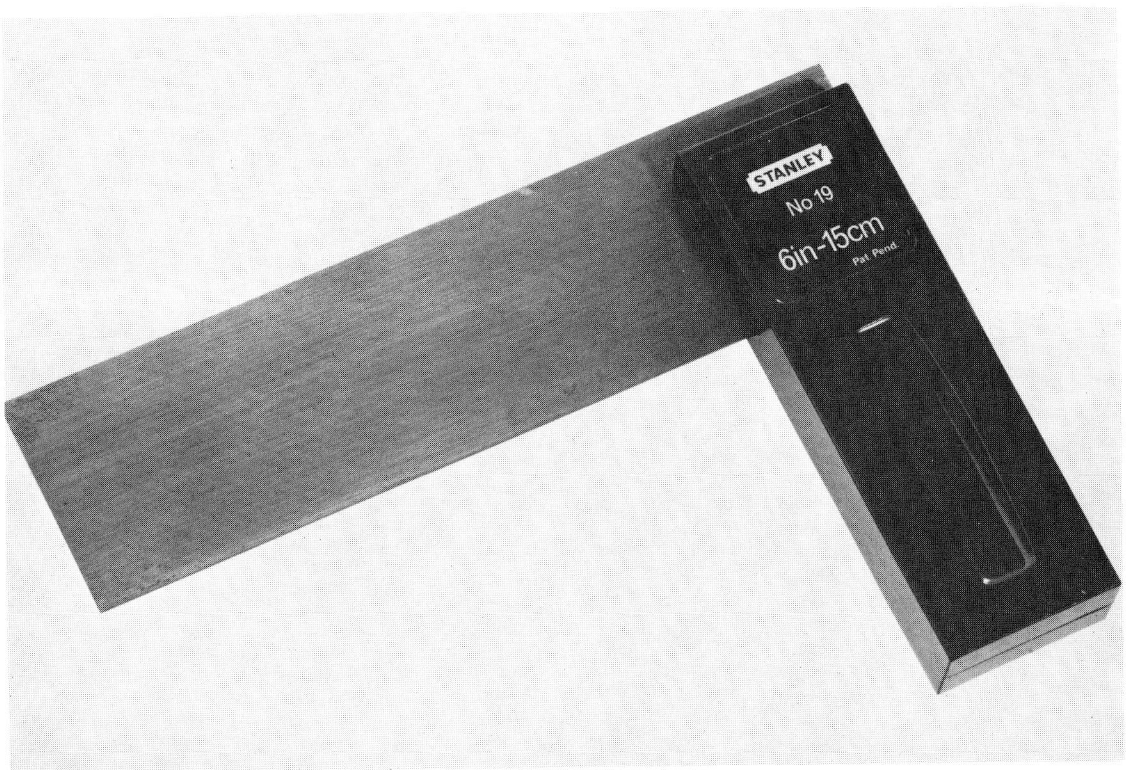

Fig. 21 (Below) Try square.

Fig. 22

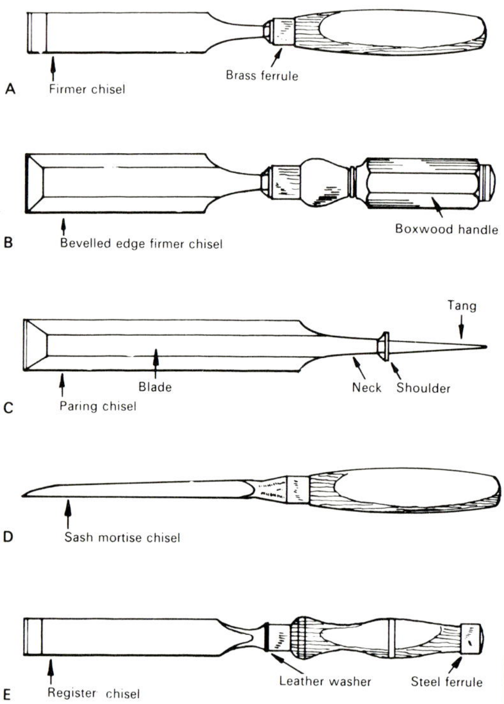

Fig. 25

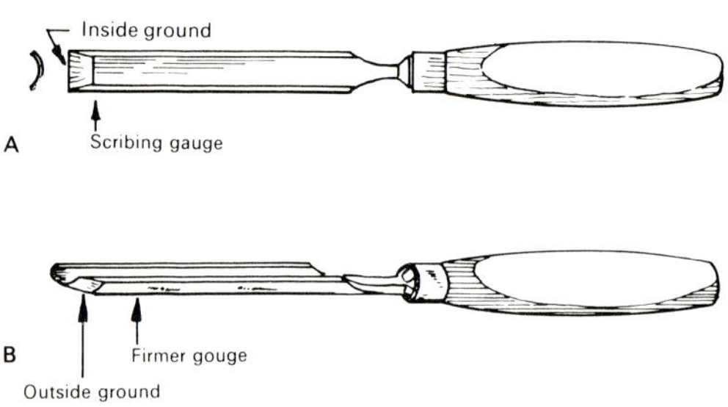

Fig. 26

Fig. 23

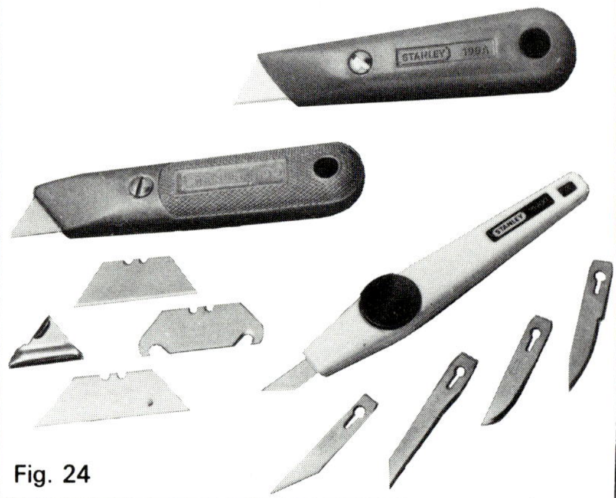

Fig. 24

Fig. 22 Combination square.

Fig. 23 Marking gauge.

Fig. 24 Range of Stanley knives.

and for marking out. A useful size is 150mm. (6in.).

Combination square: A popular size for a combination square is 150mm. (6in.). It can also be used as a depth gauge, mitre square and for testing rebates, see Fig. 22.

Marking gauge: For making cut lines down the length and across the ends of material. Shown in Fig. 23.

Cutting gauge: Similar to the marking gauge but has a small cutter in place of the spur, specially shaped to cut across the grain. Used for cutting veneers, plywood and thin material.

Mortise gauge: A mortise gauge is essential for marking out mortise and tenon joints. It has two spurs, one of which can be adjusted to suit the width of the mortise chisel.

Marking knife: For making clean cut lines for shoulders, housings, and squaring up ends of material.

Trimming knife (Stanley): Useful for marking out and cutting veneers and inlay work. See Fig. 24.

Chisels and Gouges: These are used to remove waste in the shaping of wood. The term paring means the removing of wood with a chisel by means of thin shavings. Chisel sizes are based on the width of the blades, or length of the cutting edge.

Types of chisels (Fig. 25)

A **Firmer:** A strong robust chisel for general work.

B **Bevelled firmer:** Used for general bench work and for finer work such as dovetailing. This kind of chisel is recommended in preference to the firmer chisel.

C **Paring:** A paring chisel has a longer blade than the firmer types and is used by joiners, cabinet and pattern makers for fine work. A mallet should not be used on this tool.

D **Mortise:** The blade of a mortise chisel is heavier than that of other chisels. This chisel is designed to withstand both leverage and mallet blows. The type illustrated is mostly used with soft and mild working hardwood.

E **Register:** Made with an additional ferrule which is fitted to the top of the handle to resist heavy blows from mallet or hammer. This chisel is useful for all types of heavy carpentry work.

Types of Gouges

A **Scribing:** A scribing gouge is used for scribing mouldings and shaping work. See Fig. 26.

B **Firmer:** For hollowing out. A firmer gouge being of robust construction is a good tool for removing waste quickly from large carvings or sculptures, before finishing the work with finer carving gouges.

See page 38 for range of carving tools.

Sharpening

Saws: Need to be sharpened and maintained in excellent cutting condition. Craftsmen usually sharpen their own. As it requires skill and practice the amateur is recommended to have his saws sharpened by an expert and to develop this skill by practising sharpening on an old saw.

Grinding and Sharpening of Edge Tools: At the beginning of the chapter reference was made to the advisability of purchasing only the very best quality tools. It is also necessary to be able to produce a keen cutting edge on tools and to maintain them in good working order. The grinding and sharpening of edge tools is of paramount importance to the craftsman. Sharp tools are essential for the production of good work.

Grinding: Should be done on a wet grindstone which will not overheat the tool and thus 'draw the temper' of the steel. The use of the emery wheel for quick results should be avoided.

Grinding angle: A grinding angle of 20°-25° should be maintained so that only a small amount of the sharpening bevel is left to hone on the oilstone. See diagram Fig. 27.

Sharpening: To begin with, two oilstones are an advantage, a medium grade India, an artificial stone for general work; and a fine grade Washita, a natural stone for obtaining a really keen edge. Lubricate the stone with olive oil, or a light grade machine oil; never use linseed oil, which forms a skin and clogs the stone.

Slip stones: These are necessary for sharpening both carving and scribing gouges and can be purchased in a variety of shapes and sizes. See Fig. 28, page 32.

Sharpening angle: Place the plane iron or chisel on the oilstone as shown in Fig. 28 and 29. The angle should be about 30°, maintain this angle and work back and forth several times. This action produces a sharp angle but also forms a burr or wire edge, which is removed by rubbing the back of the plane iron or chisel on the oilstone. When removing this wire edge it is essential to keep the back of the blade flat on the stone as shown in Fig. 30. Strop on a piece of supple leather to obtain a keen cutting edge.

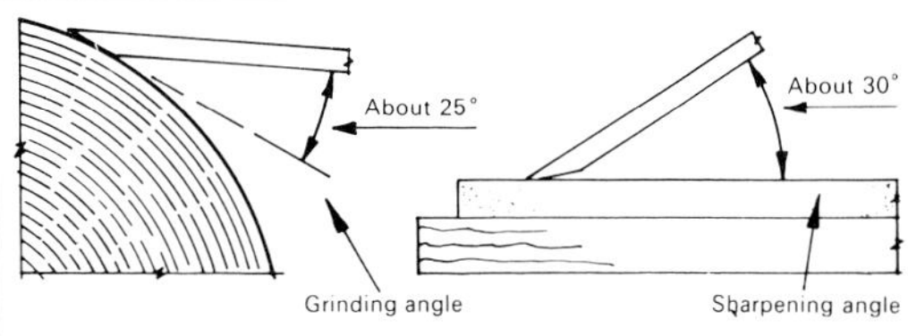

Fig. 27

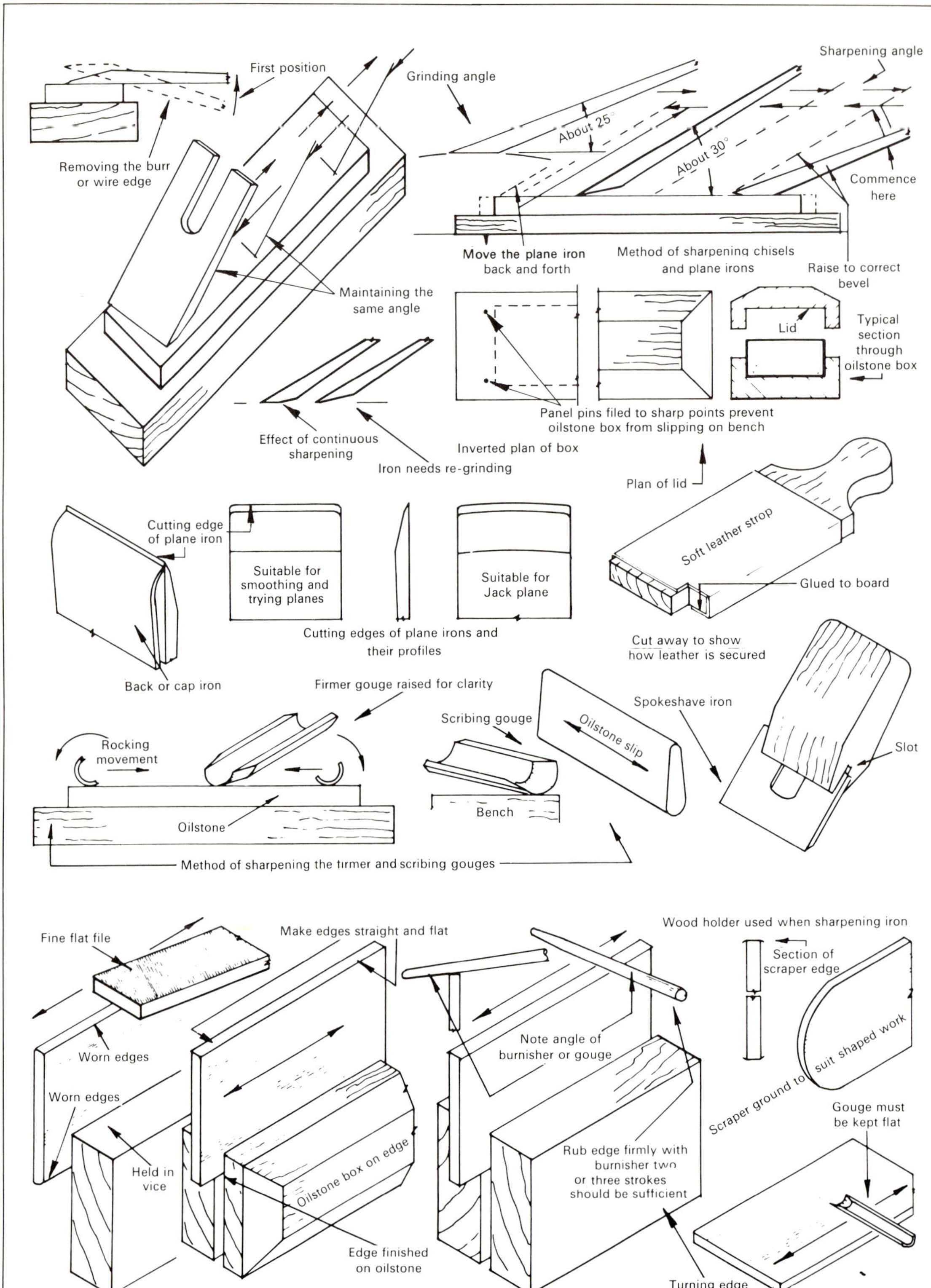
First position
Removing the burr or wire edge
Grinding angle
Maintaining the same angle
Effect of continuous sharpening
Iron needs re-grinding
Sharpening angle
About 25°
About 30°
Commence here
Move the plane iron back and forth
Method of sharpening chisels and plane irons
Raise to correct bevel
Lid
Typical section through oilstone box
Panel pins filed to sharp points prevent oilstone box from slipping on bench
Inverted plan of box
Plan of lid
Soft leather strop
Glued to board
Cut away to show how leather is secured
Cutting edge of plane iron
Back or cap iron
Suitable for smoothing and trying planes
Suitable for Jack plane
Cutting edges of plane irons and their profiles
Firmer gouge raised for clarity
Rocking movement
Oilstone
Scribing gouge
Bench
Oilstone slip
Spokeshave iron
Slot
Method of sharpening the firmer and scribing gouges
Fine flat file
Worn edges
Worn edges
Held in vice
Make edges straight and flat
Oilstone box on edge
Edge finished on oilstone
Note angle of burnisher or gouge
Rub edge firmly with burnisher two or three strokes should be sufficient
Turning edge of scraper
Wood holder used when sharpening iron
Section of scraper edge
Scraper ground to suit shaped work
Gouge must be kept flat
Rubbing down ends

Fig. 28

Fig. 29 (Above) Sharpening a plane iron.

Fig. 30 (Below) Removing the wire edge.

Useful hints

1. Never hold an oilstone in the vice. It is better to make a box for it.

2. When sharpening, use the full length of the stone. Small wood blocks 'let in' at each end of the stone enable this to be done.

3. When sharpening small chisels, do not use only the centre of the stone otherwise the stone will be worn hollow, but move the blade from side to side so as to use the entire surface.

4. Two small pins driven in the bottom of one end of the oilstone box, with their heads filed off to points, will prevent the box slipping on the bench when in use.

5. Keep the oilstone clean and the oil from drying out by replacing the lid after use.

Sharpening gouges

Firmer gouge: This is sharpened on the oilstone with a rocking movement so that every part of the bevel is rubbed evenly. The burr is removed with an oilstone slip. See Fig. 28, page 32.

Scribing gouge: Sharpened with the oilstone slip and has the burr taken off by rocking the outer surface flat on the oilstone. See Fig. 28, page 32.

Sharpening a scraper: This is illustrated by Fig. 28, page 32.

Boring tools

Brace: That shown in Fig. 31 is commonly known as the carpenter's brace or sway. The chuck is designed to hold the various bits used by the woodworker. Braces are made in three sweep sizes, 203mm. (8in.), 250mm. (10in.), and 305mm. (12in.) and are of plain or ratchet type.

Wheel brace or hand drill: A very efficient tool, a wheel brace, Fig. 31, is designed to hold a range of twist drills and countersinks. Twist drills are used mainly for making holes for screws and small bolts.

Archimedean and push drills: Very useful for making small holes in plywood, mouldings and thin wood, when using panel pins or fine screws. The drill points are stronger than twist drills of the same size.

Bradawl: This is a most useful tool for making small holes for screws and nails. It should be kept sharp by filing. Note that in use boring must commence with the blade across the grain.

Twist bits: That given in Fig. 31 is used for the accurate boring of holes. The dowel bit is shorter than the standard pattern.

Forstner bit: Bores holes with smooth sides and flat bottom, see Fig. 32.

Centre bits: Used for boring holes in thin material.

Countersinks: For the countersinking of holes to take screw heads.

Shell and Cobra bits: The twist drill has largely superseded this type of bit, although owing to their strength and flexibility they are still favoured by the boatbuilder.

'Flat bit': One of many useful types which can be used in an electric drill, see Fig. 32.

Miscellaneous tools

Hammer: Used chiefly for driving in nails. The Warrington is favoured by joiners and cabinet-makers. The claw hammer is popular with carpenters because of the ease with which nails can be withdrawn with its claw.

Mallets: Used for striking handles of chisels, gouges, when hand pressure is not sufficient. This tool is often used when assembling framing.

Carving Mallets: Their special advantage is that any part of the head can be used. More suitable when carving than the ordinary type. See page 39.

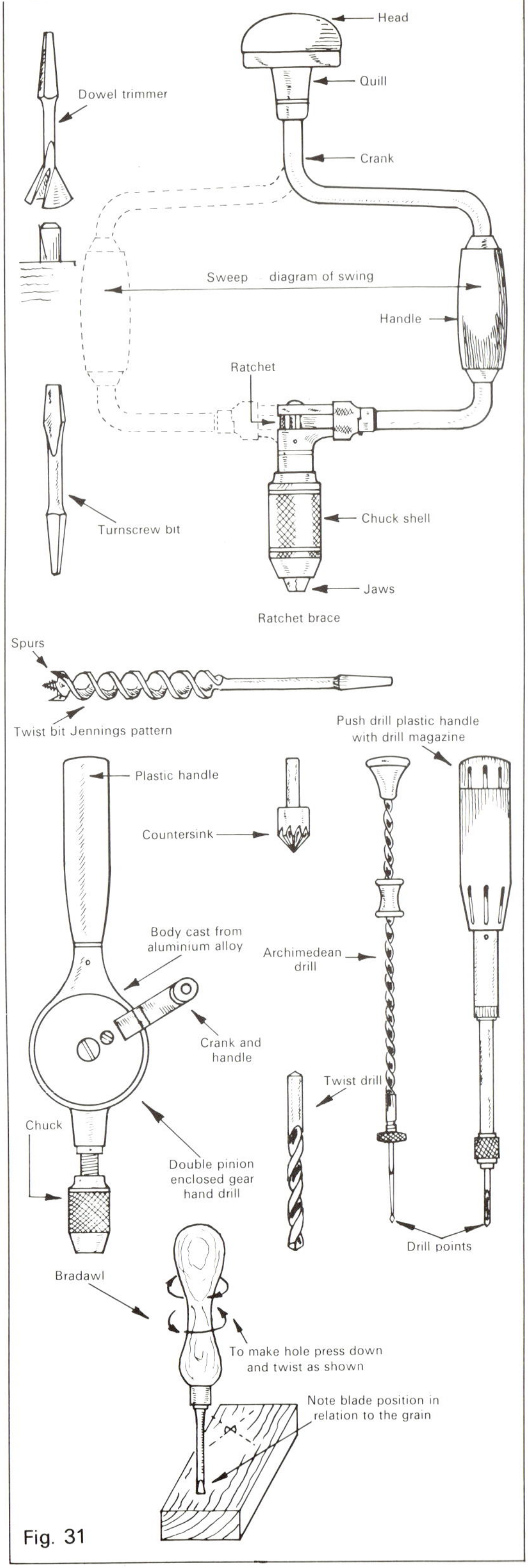

Fig. 31

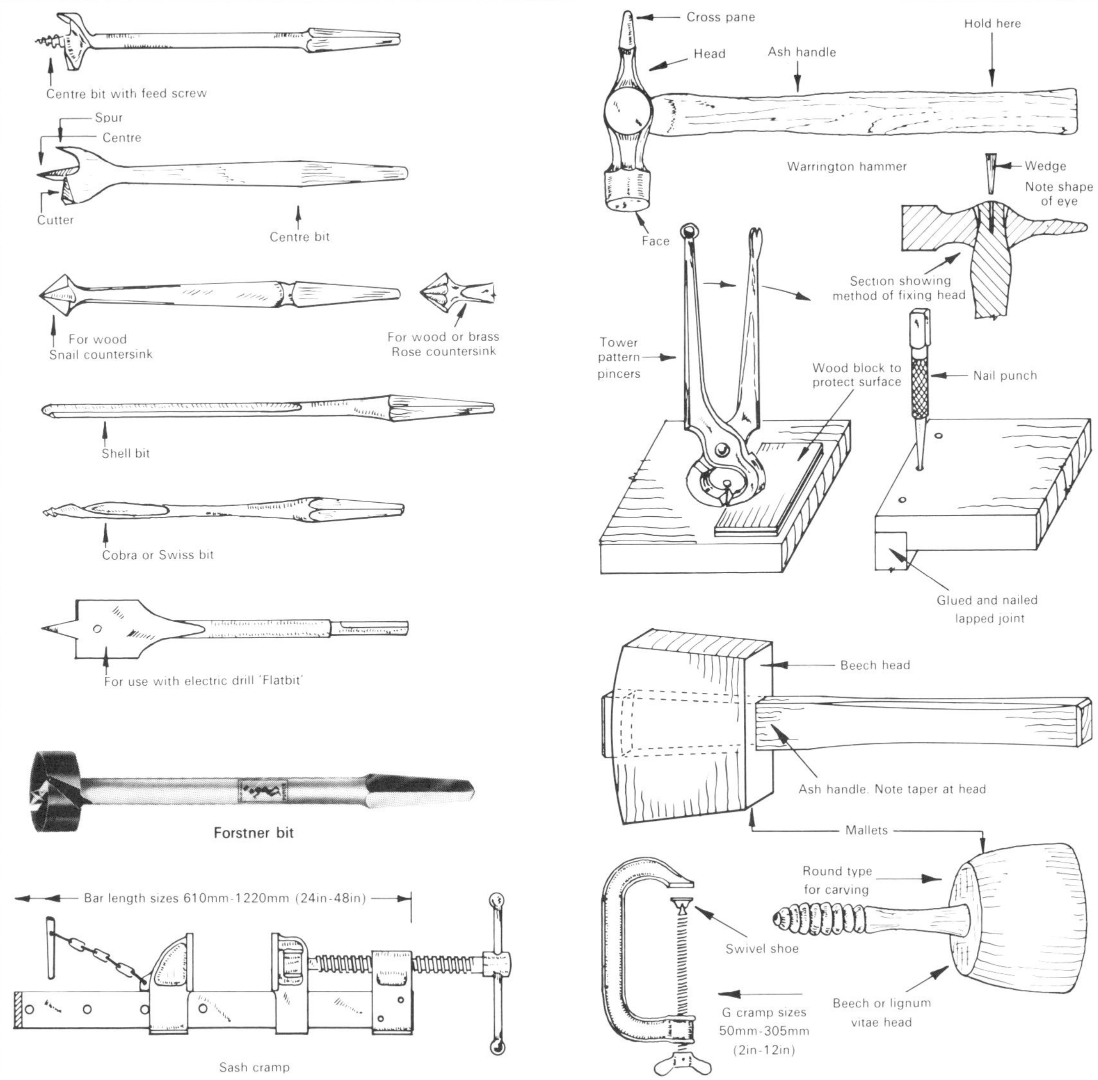

Fig. 32

Screwdrivers: Useful sizes and types of screwdrivers are, 203mm. (8in.) cabinet pattern Fig. 33 (right), 150mm. (6in.) ratchet pattern. Fig. 34 shows a range of Pozidrive screwdrivers. Screwdrivers are often neglected, resulting in damaged wood and screw heads. They should be made to fit the slot and should be slightly smaller in width than the screw head.

Nail Punch: For sinking nail heads below the surface of the wood.

Pincers: For withdrawing bent nails. A Tower pattern is recommended.

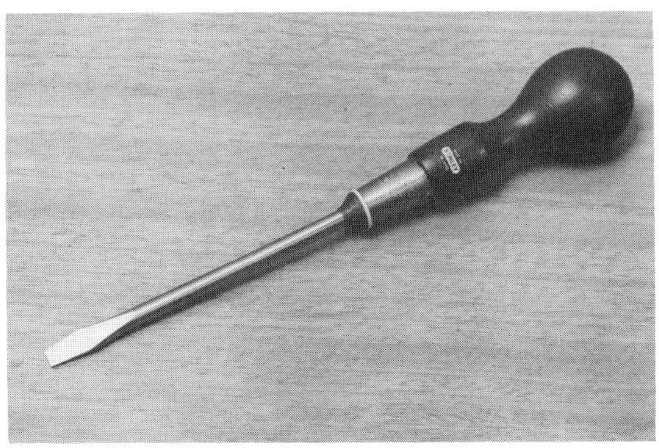

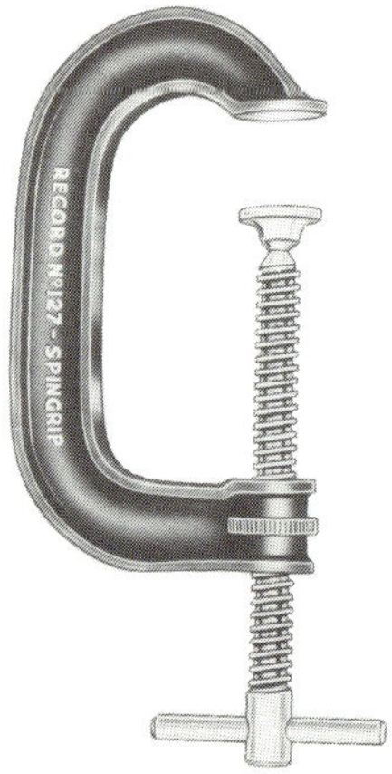

Fig. 35

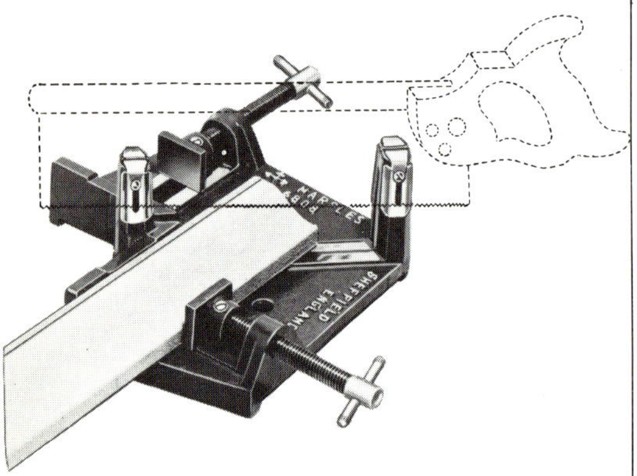

Fig. 36

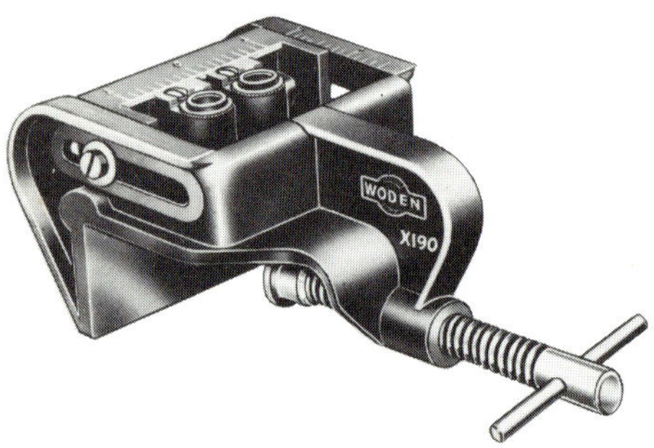

Fig. 37

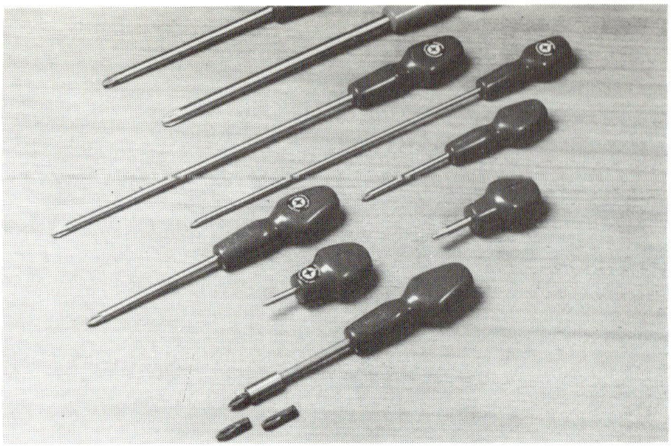

'G' Cramps: Used for cramping up and holding work secure while shaping. Useful sizes are, 50mm. (2in.) to about 203mm. (8in.). See Fig. 35.

Sash Cramps: Used for cramping up doors, frames, panels, sashes and carcases. Useful sizes are 610mm. (24in.), 915mm. (36in.), 1220mm. (48in.). See Fig. 36 and page 41, showing dolphin in sash cramp.

Fig. 34 (Above right) Pozidrive screwdrivers.

Fig. 35 'G' cramp with fine adjustment.

Fig. 36 Mitre cutter and cramp.

Fig. 37 Dowelling jig.

Fig. 38 (Opp. above) Various workshop-made tools. Back left to right: centre square, winding strips, small centre square, tee gauge. Front: veneer hammer, box square and mitre template.

Fig. 39 (Opp. below) Mitre shooting block. In the foreground is a picture frame showing tourniquet and veneer keys to secure mitre joints.

Carving tools

There is a wide range of carving tools available of which a few are shown on these pages. Professional carvers may have up to eighty or more various carving tools in their kit, but of this large number of tools, the carver, on the average job, may use only about twenty, the others being necessary only when special and intricate work is being executed.

Carving tools are graded by width, in sizes varying from $1\frac{1}{2}$mm. ($\frac{1}{16}$in.) to 25mm. (1in.) and manufacturers invariably have their own code of letters or numbers to distinguish the various patterns and shapes, and this can be somewhat confusing for the beginner. To enable the novice to select economically a suitable range of tools catering for a good variety of work, the author has recommended the following as a basic kit of carving tools. Others can be added when, through experience, more advanced work can be attempted.

M1 Square chisel 6mm($\frac{1}{4}$in) 9mm($\frac{3}{8}$in) 12mm($\frac{1}{2}$in)

M2 Skew chisel 6mm($\frac{1}{4}$in) 9mm($\frac{3}{8}$in) 12mm($\frac{1}{2}$in)

M3 – M11 Straight gouge

3mm ($\frac{1}{8}$in) 6mm ($\frac{1}{4}$in) 9mm ($\frac{3}{8}$in) 12mm ($\frac{1}{2}$in) 15mm ($\frac{5}{8}$in)

M5, M6, M7, M8, M11

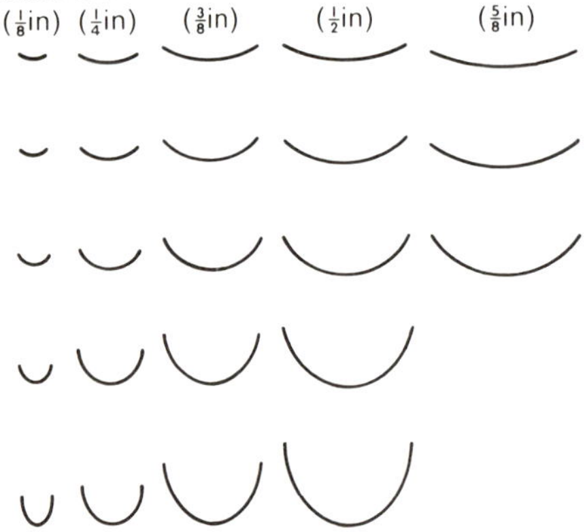

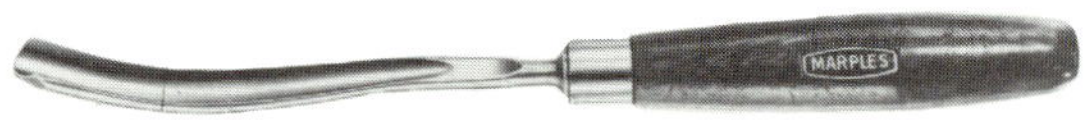

M14 – M16 Curved gouge

3mm ($\frac{1}{8}$in) 6mm ($\frac{1}{4}$in) 9mm ($\frac{3}{8}$in) 12mm ($\frac{1}{2}$in) 15mm ($\frac{5}{8}$in)

M14, M16

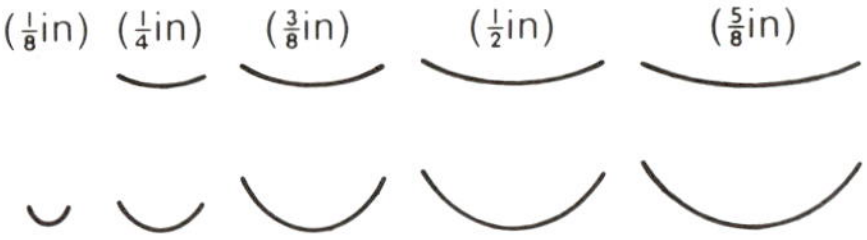

M21 Spoon bit chisel, square 3mm($\frac{1}{8}$in) 6mm($\frac{1}{4}$in)

M39 Straight V parting tool

3mm ($\frac{1}{8}$in) 6mm ($\frac{1}{4}$in) 9mm ($\frac{3}{8}$in) 12mm ($\frac{1}{2}$in)

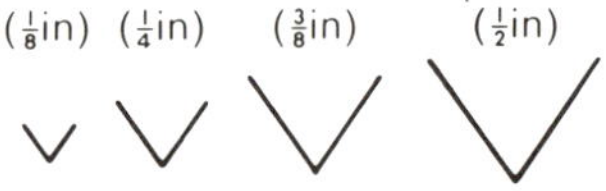

M47 Veiner $1\frac{1}{2}$mm($\frac{1}{16}$in)

M1 square chisel, 6mm. ($\frac{1}{4}$in.)
M2 skew chisel 9mm. ($\frac{3}{8}$in.)
M3 straight gouge 12.5mm. ($\frac{1}{2}$in.)
M5 straight gouge 12.5mm. ($\frac{1}{2}$in.)
M7 straight gouge 16mm. ($\frac{5}{8}$in.)
M11 straight gouge 6mm. ($\frac{1}{4}$in.)
M14 curved gouge 12.5mm. ($\frac{1}{2}$in.)
M39 straight parting tool 9mm. ($\frac{3}{8}$in.)
M47 Veiner 1.5mm. ($\frac{1}{16}$in.)
A carving mallet
203mm. (8in.) wood rasps and files, rifflers, Surform tools and scrapers

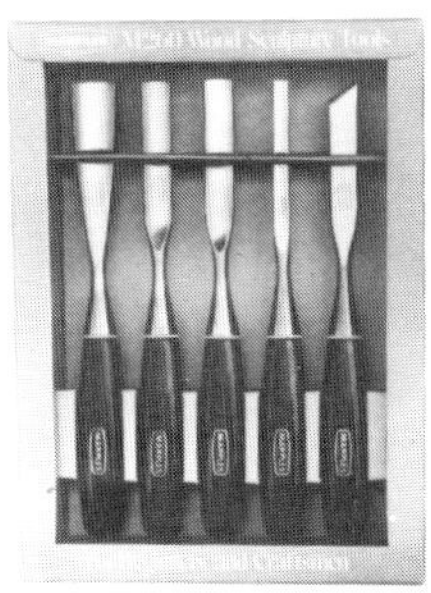

Fig. 47 Marples set of Blue Chip wood sculpture chisel and gouges.

Fig. 48 Draw knife.

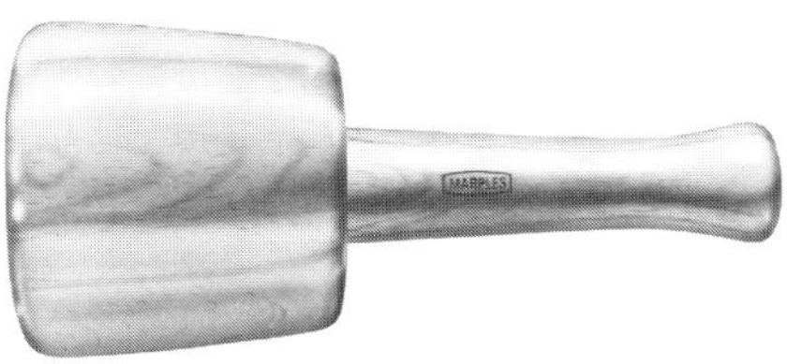

Fig. 49 Carving mallet.

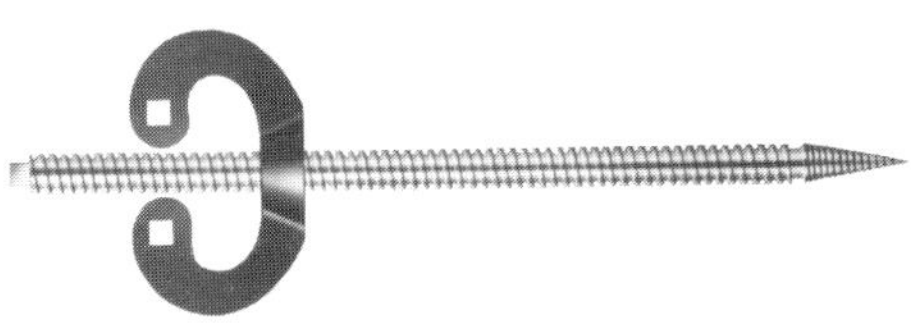

Fig. 50 Woodcarver's screw.

For large sculptures, a heavier type of gouge may be needed to remove the majority of the waste and the Marples M260 range of wood sculpture gouges is recommended. A draw knife, Fig. 48, is also useful for the quick removal of waste.

Sharpening of carving tools

To produce a really keen edge on carving tools it is necessary to finish by stropping on a piece of leather which has been impregnated with a mixture of emery powder (flour grade) or pumice powder and Vaseline. For general information see page 32.

Slip stones: Made in various shapes and sizes, and are essential when sharpening gouges and Vee tools.
Fluter or Veiner: A narrow, deep gouge; a fine edged slip stone is needed to remove the wire edge when sharpening.
Sharpening the Vee or parting tool: A three cornered or triangular slip stone is needed.
Gouges: These are sharpened so that they are kept square across the end. Some carvers prefer to make a small second bevel on the hollow side.
Carving chisels: Have a bevel on both sides and the cutting edge should be kept straight.

Note. A sharp gouge should make a clean cut across the grain of hard or soft wood, leaving a shiny, burnished-looking surface. To protect the cutting edges of your carving tools, keep them in a baize roll when not in use.

Bench: Although a certain amount of wood carving can be executed successfully on a strong kitchen table, a good bench is essential for the professional and keen amateur craftsman. See photograph, Fig. 51.
Holding devices: Securing a carving firmly so that it can be worked on often presents problems. The carver plans ahead, assesses the likely difficulties and where necessary makes use of a vice, G cramps, bench-holdfasts and woodcarver's screw. (See Fig. 50.) A wood block, glued and screwed to the base of the subject is a simple and effective method of securing a job, see Fig. 54. Securing work in a heavy sash cramp is

another useful method. See photograph of Dolphin page 41. Flat panels for relief carving can be secured by screwing strips of wood to a board and fixing the panel with folding wedges. See photograph page 44.

Safety factors

Use only sharp tools and make sure the work is firmly secured when using gouges or other tools. If there is any danger of chips flying off the gouge or chisel, it is advisable to wear goggles to protect your eyes.

Keep your hands behind the cutting edge when using edge tools. Wash your hands thoroughly after using modern glues to safeguard against skin irritation.

Fig. 51 Emir bench No. 1202. By courtesy of Emmerich (Berlon) Ltd.

Fig. 52 Bird with fish. This was held securely by a carver's screw. A block of wood screwed to the base would also enable it to be held securely in the vice.

Fig. 53 Dolphin near completion. Note the extra length allowed for cramping.

Fig. 54 Feeding time. Group of birds showing a screw in the base which allows the sculpture to be turned around as well as holding it firmly in the vice.

Fig. 52

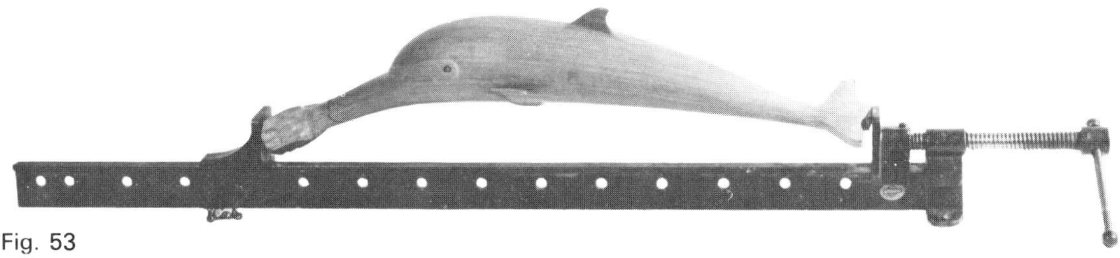

Fig. 53

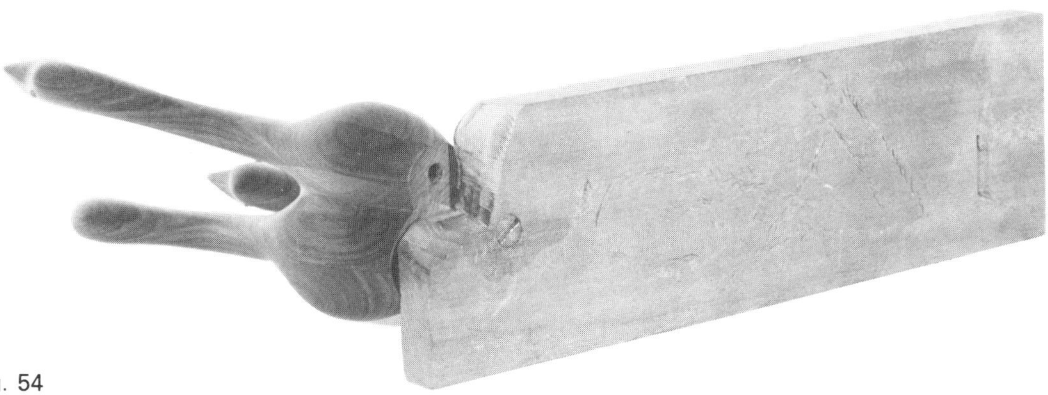

Fig. 54

BASIC DESIGNS AND TECHNIQUES

This section has been planned to incorporate basic design and techniques as a foundation for more adventurous work. As far as possible an attempt has been made to arrange the material progressively, so that the reader may be stimulated in design awareness, develop skill in the manipulation of the various woodworking tools and progress at his or her own pace.

Nature continually surprises us with its infinite range of beauty. The colours and forms of nature have always been a source of inspiration to the artist and designer craftsman: the sky with its ever-changing patterns of cloud formation and colour; sea and shore; animal and bird life; the proportions of the human form; trees, flowers and insects; all contribute to inspire the imagination and provide a source from which ideas can be formulated when designing. One can also admire the grace of a ship, the billowing sails of a racing yacht, the lines of the 'Concorde' or the stream-lines of a racing car.

Form is all around us, we should observe, sketch, make models and try to develop an eye for line and proportion and an appreciation of colour harmony. Endeavour to harness a little of this beauty and make it work for you. Use your sketch book to build up a rich store of information.

This section begins with the designing and making of plaques in plywood and progresses through an interesting variety of pleasing works of artistic merit, which include basic foundation requirements. The following techniques are included in this range: marking out and cutting plywood, basic sawing, planing, chiselling, boring of holes, shaping of wood and the use of carving gouges, wood rasps and files, scrapers and sandpaper.

Practice in the use of the Vee tool and fluter or Veiner gouge is suggested. Practice is similarly recommended in using the scratch stock for simple mouldings and inlay work and the making of decorative stop chamfers for church work.

Mentioned too are the various backgrounds for the display of work, such as hessian, cork, veneered panels, framed work as well as the mounting of sculpture on plinths and stainless steel rods and the building up of relief panels with applied ornamentation.

A fairly wide variety of woods have been used in the making of the artefacts in this book. It is only by actually working in a variety of woods that you can establish a sound knowledge of timber, its workability, colour, grain, aroma, tactile and other qualities.

Each photograph has an explanatory caption giving as much information as possible on the subject. Where appropriate the various finishes will be mentioned.

Chip carving

This is one of the oldest forms of carving and it is still practised, although the demand is somewhat limited today. Very few tools are required to produce this type of carving, as most work can be done with a knife or chisel. On some patterns a gouge may be necessary to complete the decoration. The basic cuts, which are made with the chisel, are of a triangular or three-sided formation.

Special features and suggestions: This form of decoration has great possibilities if used with restraint. Try designing and making simple chip carving decoration on mirror frames, book ends, spice racks and bread boards. Fig. 1 shows a sampler with a few patterns; practise these cuts on a piece of lime or sycamore.

Incised carving

This is basically cutting into the surface of a piece of wood with a Vee tool or Veiner gouge, to form various designs and patterns. This type of carving offers considerable scope in the designing of geometrical patterns, flower arrangements, landscapes and lettering.

Special features and suggestions: Make a few practice cuts with your Vee tool. Hold it firmly with one hand, with the wrist resting on the work, guide the Vee tool into the wood tapping the handle with a mallet in a series of short, quick blows.

Design a flower arrangement which is to be incised into a plaque made out of 12mm. ($\frac{1}{2}$in.) thick birch plywood. To equalize the pull and prevent the plaque from warping, it is to be veneered on both sides with a dark contrasting wood, such as walnut, teak, rosewood or utile.

Try incising (cutting in) a name or number on a piece of hardwood; this would look equally well if executed with a Vee tool or a Veiner gouge. The photographs Fig. 2 and 3 are examples of incised carving.

Relief carving

This is the adornment of a surface in which the subject or image stands out in relief from a background. It is the varying depths and shaping that produces the effective and pleasing shadow contrasts which give this type of carving its particular charm. The main forms are as follows:

High relief carving (Haut-relief)

This form of carving can have an almost three-dimensional appeal. It is well defined and stands out prominently from the background, which is usually an integral part of it. The various depths of the shaping and the undercutting, which can be achieved in this type of carving, are very satisfying to the artist craftsman. See Fig. 4.

Low relief carving (Bas-relief)

With low relief, the depth and contrast between the subject and the background is less prominent. When the design is cut completely into the surface of the wood it is described as hollow relief or intaglio. Another form of 'low relief' is demonstrated when a subject is cut separately to an outline—for example a fish, a horse or bird—as illustrated by Fig. 18, page 49, then carved to a final shape or form and applied to a background.

When the work is pierced and carved as for church screens or doors, it comes under the category of relief carving.

Wood sculpture

This is three-dimensional work or carving in the round as shown in Fig. 6. The subject should stand alone and look right—visually pleasing—when viewed from any angle, good form is essential. When developing a sculpture it is often necessary to prepare numerous sketches and a model in clay or Polystyrene. A knowledge of anatomy both human and animal is an advantage, and it is a good idea to look at books dealing with the subject.

Direct carving

Some sculptors prefer to discover their subject when working directly into the wood, as opposed to the more conventional method of preparation.

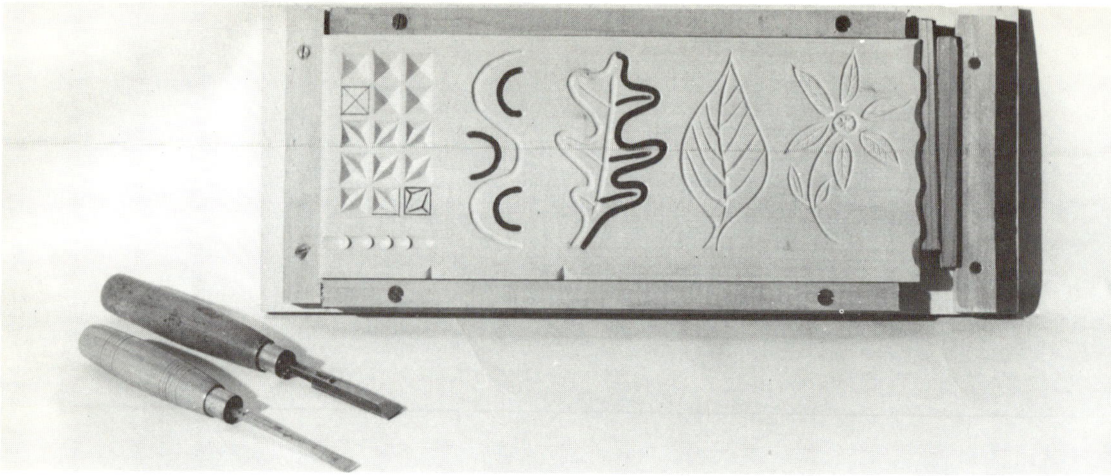

Fig. 1 (Top) Sampler in lime wood 350mm × 140mm × 25mm ($13\frac{3}{4}$in × $5\frac{1}{2}$in × 1in). On the left is shown the setting out and cutting of suitable patterns for chip carving. These are easily produced using a bevelled edge chisel or a spade-shaped carver's chisel (foreground). Size of chisel illustrated is 12mm ($\frac{1}{2}$in). Also shown is a pleasing pattern made with a 9mm ($\frac{3}{8}$in) carving gouge. The leaf and flower designs on the right were made with a Vee tool, while the partly-painted designs are made with the Veiner gouge. On the right is a pair of folding wedges which secure the panel.

Fig. 2 Freesias. Incised carving 400mm × 200mm ($15\frac{3}{4}$in × $7\frac{7}{8}$in) on 12mm ($\frac{1}{2}$in) plywood veneered with rosewood. The panel can be finished either with French polish or a sanding sealer, lightly rubbed down and finally waxed.

Fig. 3 (Right) Demonstration name plates in lime. Incised with the Vee tool (foreground).

Fig. 4

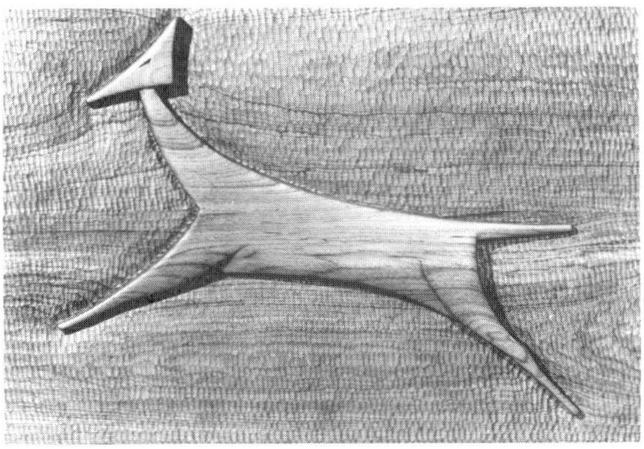

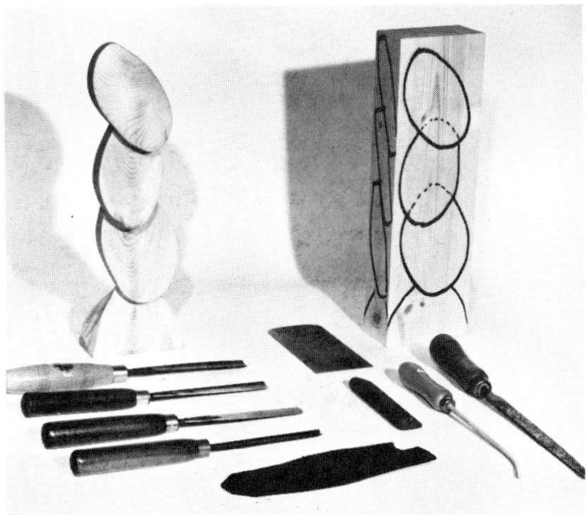

Fig. 4 Swan in flight. A good example of high relief carving. The material used was a piece of waney-edged yew, 790mm × 280mm × 50mm (31⅛in × 11in × 2in). Parts of the body and wings are undercut to accentuate the form and to give a feeling of movement. The grain, knots, sapwood and the natural outline of the timber all contribute to make this an aesthetically pleasing carving. The majority of the background is left from the tool. It is finished with linseed oil treatment.

Fig. 5 (Left) Animal form. A fine example of low relief carving in teak. The carving stands out sufficiently to give a good, clean outline. The background is finished 'left from the tool' giving a pleasant and contrasting finish. The panel is finished with a wax treatment. Made by a student of Shoreditch College.

Fig. 6 (Right) Cactus. Wood form in Scots pine 300mm × 100mm × 50mm (11¾in × 4in × 2in). A carving suitable for beginners, showing the three-dimensional aspect of sculpture. Note the marking out on the material and some of the tools used for shaping and completing the form. This was finished with two applications of Petroleum jelly rubbed well into the wood. The tools are top left and working down: carving gouges; 12mm (½in) No. 7 straight gouge; 12mm (½in) No. 6 straight gouge; 12mm (½in) No. 3 straight gouge; 9mm (⅜in) No. 8 straight gouge; centre to right: leather strop; 100mm (4in) slipstone; 127mm (5in) cabinet scraper, one end shaped; 4mm ($\frac{5}{32}$in) 'Abrafile' bent to suit shape; 152mm (6in) wood rasp.

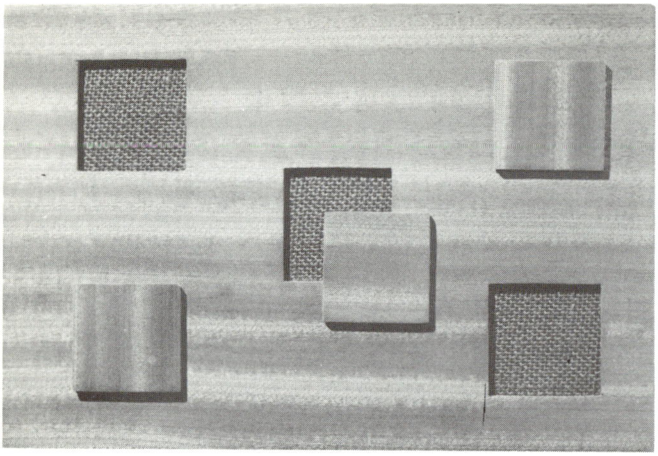

Fig. 7

Fig. 8

Fig. 9

Fig. 7 Abstract panel designed for practice in marking out, sawing and edge planing of plywood. Material required: 1 piece of 6mm ($\frac{1}{4}$in) mahogany-faced plywood 300mm × 200mm ($11\frac{3}{4}$in × $7\frac{7}{8}$in); small piece of fabric for backing. Tools: rule, try square, marking knife, tenon saw, smoothing plane, wheelbrace and drill, fretsaw, fine wood file, sandpaper, cork rubber.

Fig. 8 Abstract panel in oak-faced plywood. Try out some new ideas using leaf and animal shapes. These panels are lightly polished, rubbed down and waxed before the background is applied.

Fig. 9 Wall plaque in softwood; 460mm × 95mm × 20mm ($18\frac{1}{8}$in × $3\frac{3}{4}$in × $\frac{3}{4}$in). Mounted on an hessian-covered plywood base. Selected facets are painted black enhancing the appearance. The hessian is paper-based and is fixed on to the plaque with rubber-based glue.

Fig. 10

Fig. 11

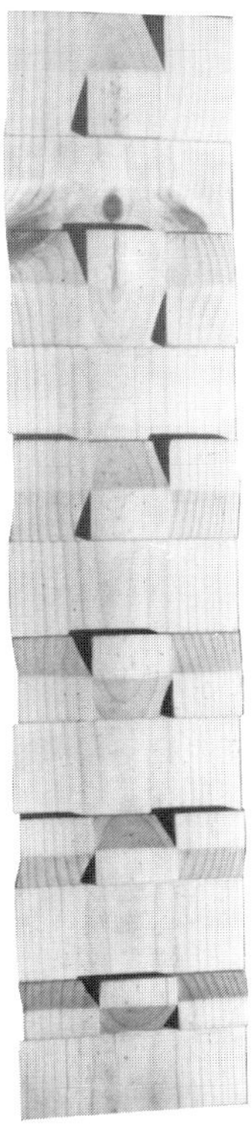

Fig. 12

Fig. 10 Shaped plywood pieces cut from 9mm ($\frac{3}{8}$in) mahogany-faced multi-plywood, the bevelled surface shaping being made with the aid of a disc sander. The finished pieces are glued to a background of mahogany-faced plywood and sealed with transparent polish.

Fig. 11 Second panel of shaped plywood pieces. The lighter-coloured core highlights the shapes and makes an attractive panel. The bevelled edges on this panel were also made with a disc sander. **Fig. 10** and **11** made by a student of Shoreditch College.

Fig. 12 Wall plaque in softwood. The grain of this piece of Scots pine shows up well on the various facets. Mainly saw and chisel work.

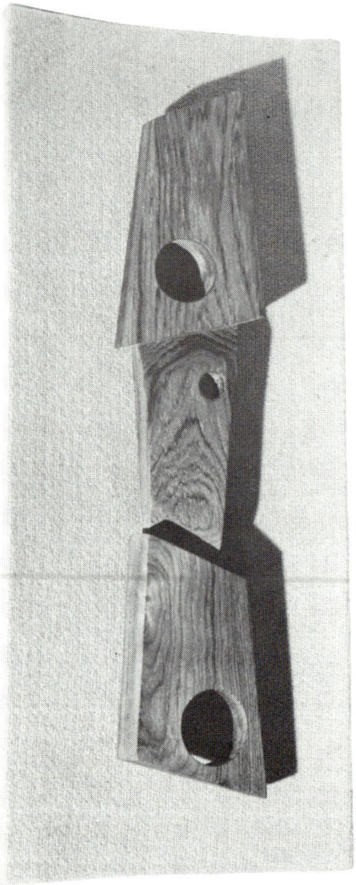

Fig. 13 (Top) Fish shape in 9mm ($\frac{3}{8}$in) plywood. Shaping plywood in this fashion brings out an infinite range of pleasing and shapely contours, these also look attractive when mounted on a base either singly or in shoals.

Fig. 14 (Below right) Candleholders in elm. These make a good test in setting out and accurate shaping. The holders are 58mm ($2\frac{1}{4}$in) square and 32mm ($1\frac{1}{4}$in) thick and are oil polished. Tools: rule, try square, marking knife, tenon saw, 18mm ($\frac{3}{4}$in) twist bit and brace, 9mm ($\frac{3}{8}$in) scribbing gouge, 32mm ($1\frac{1}{4}$in) bevelled-edged firmer chisel, smoothing and block planes.

Fig. 15 Abstract plaque in teak. The shape and arrangement of the holes in relation to the overall design makes this an interesting subject. The shapes stand away from the background, which is shaped in plan, about 9mm ($\frac{3}{8}$in). Made by a student of Shoreditch College.

Fig. 16 Plaque. Bird forms in muninga. The eyes are shaped out of end grain sycamore let in and glued. Made by a student of Shoreditch College.

Fig. 17 Abstract shapes in sequoia cut out of a 25mm (1in) thick board. The reddish colour of the timber against a suitable hessian background makes a delightful panel.

Fig. 18 Bird in flight. 330mm × 330mm (13in × 13in). The finished carving is mounted on a cork base which is glued to a 9mm ($\frac{3}{8}$in) plywood panel with an oak lipping.

Fig. 17

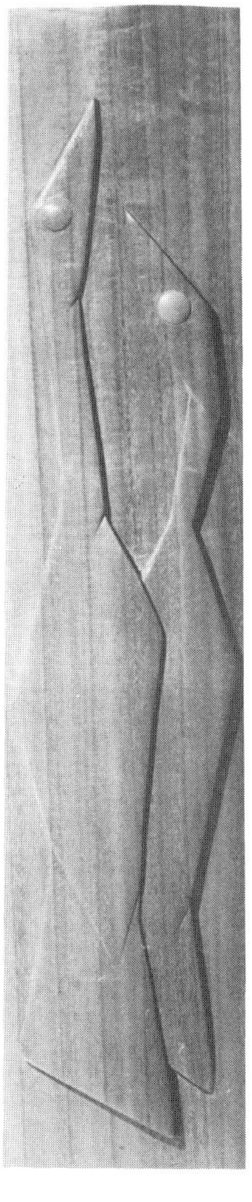

Fig. 16

Fig. 18

Fig. 19 Bird and dolphin cut and shaped out of 12mm ($\frac{1}{2}$in) plywood. The bird is left as finished from the carving gouge which gives a realistic, feather-like appearance. The dolphin has been cleaned up smooth and finished with a fine grade of sandpaper. Both carvings have been lightly French polished and have a matt finish.

Fig. 20 (Below) Design sketches for various projects.

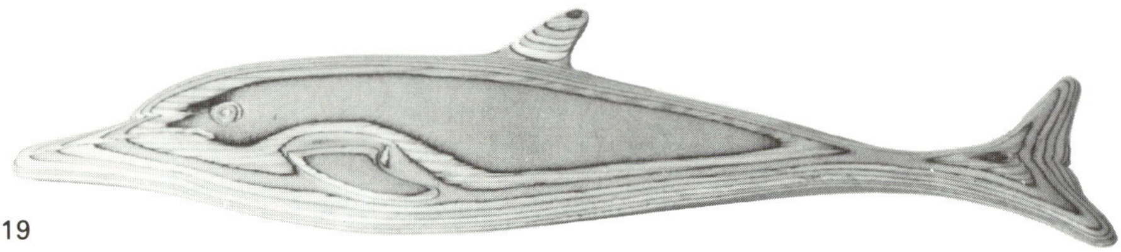

Fig. 19

Fig. 21 Teak plaque with parabolic curves. This makes an excellent subject for the beginner as it can be shaped with a 12mm ($\frac{1}{2}$in) M7 straight gouge. The curves are drawn free-hand and spaced by eye only.

Fig. 22–24 Three views of a dish in African walnut. **Fig. 22** shows the marking out, preliminary outline cuts with a Veiner gouge and removal of waste. When the recesses are worked down to the required depth, smooth out with a flatter gouge, scrape and finally sandpaper. Work of this nature can be held firmly to the bench with a 'G' cramp or bench holdfast. Complete inside shaping before cutting to outline, then clean up edges with a spokeshave. Reverse and carefully sculpture underside as shown. This dish was finished with a linseed oil treatment.

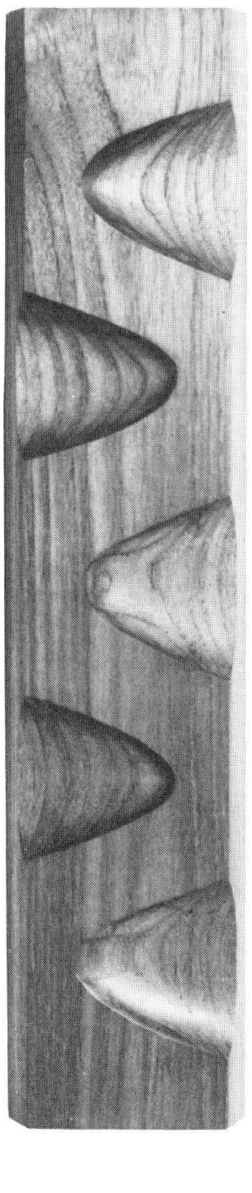

Fig. 21

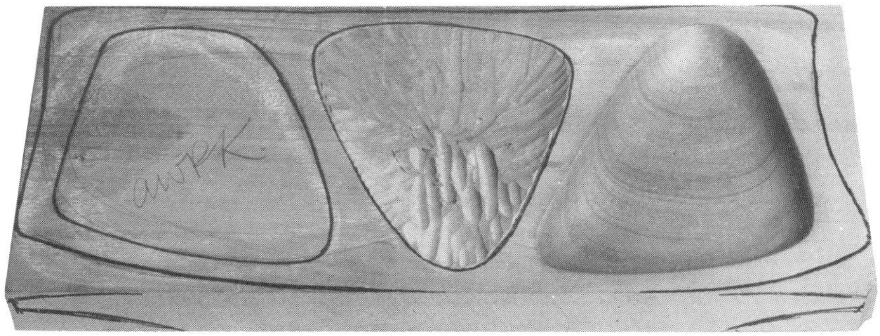

Fig. 22

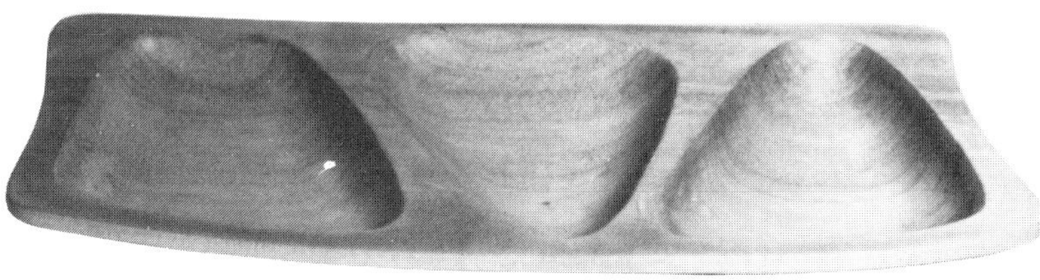

Fig. 23

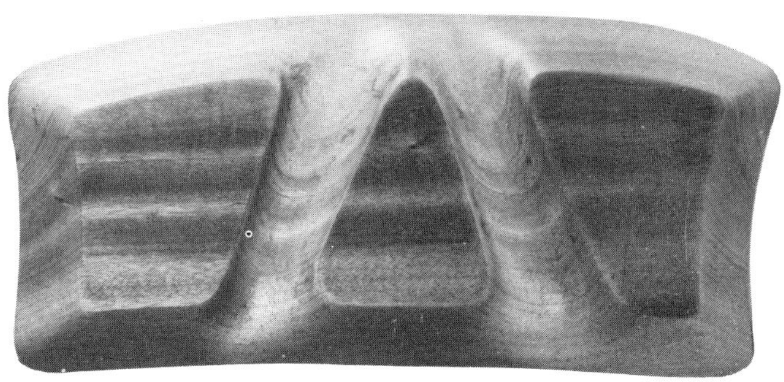

Fig. 24

Various stages in making a shaped dish

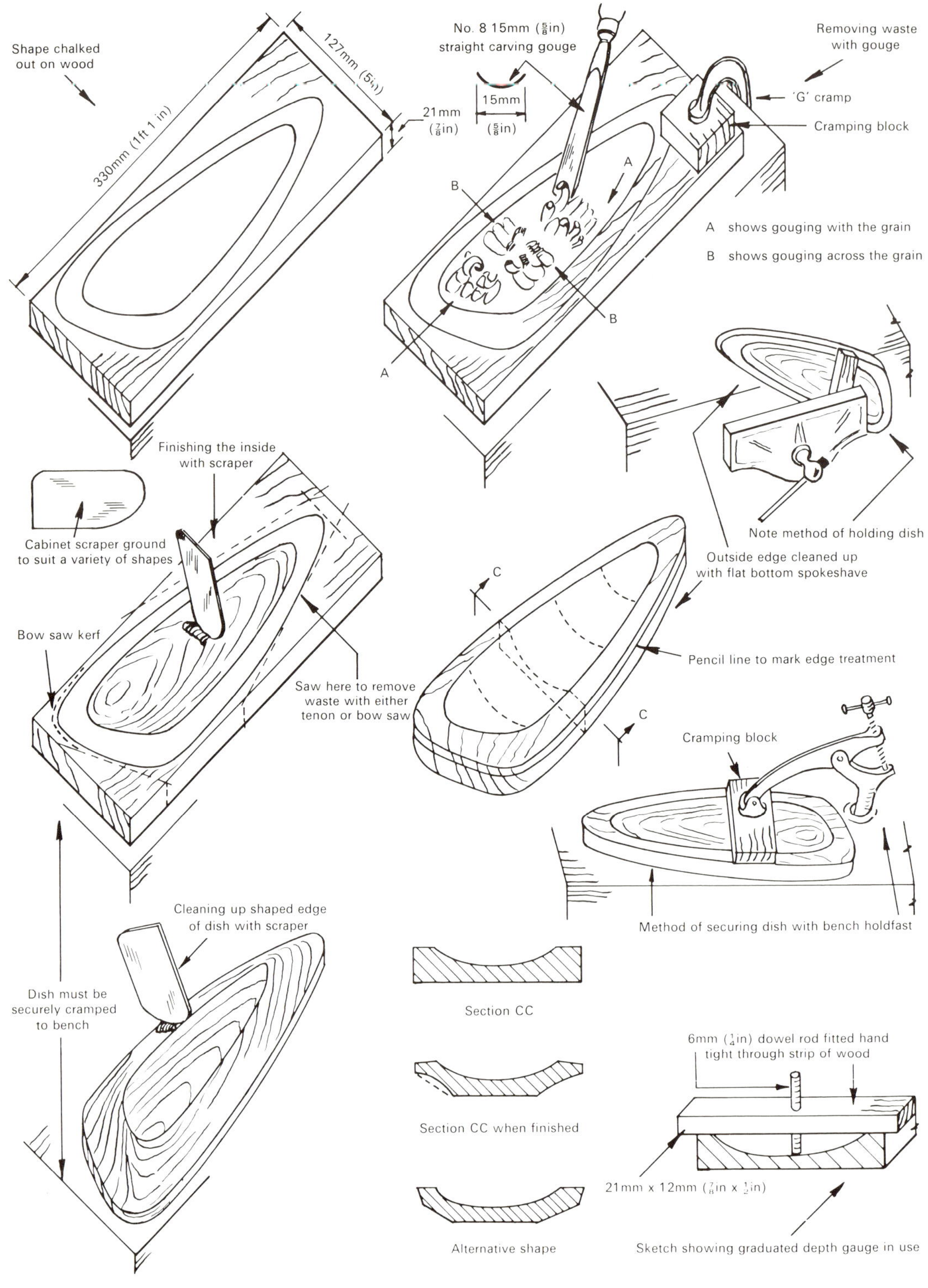

Fig. 25 Three shaped dishes. The central one is in rosewood, the others in African walnut.

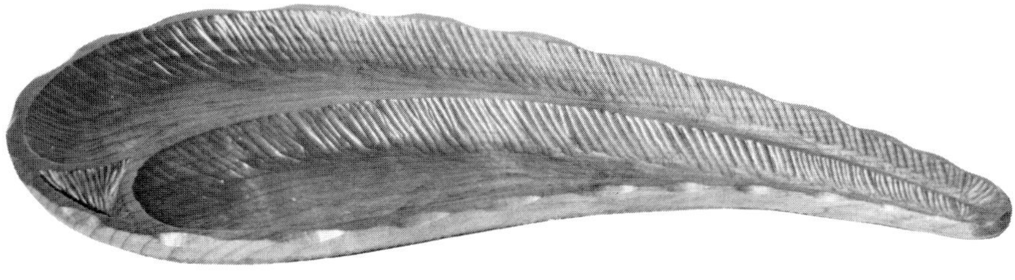

Fig. 26 Dish in cherrywood. Carved out of a 25mm (1in) thick board and left finished as from the tool. It was finally linseed oiled and burnished.

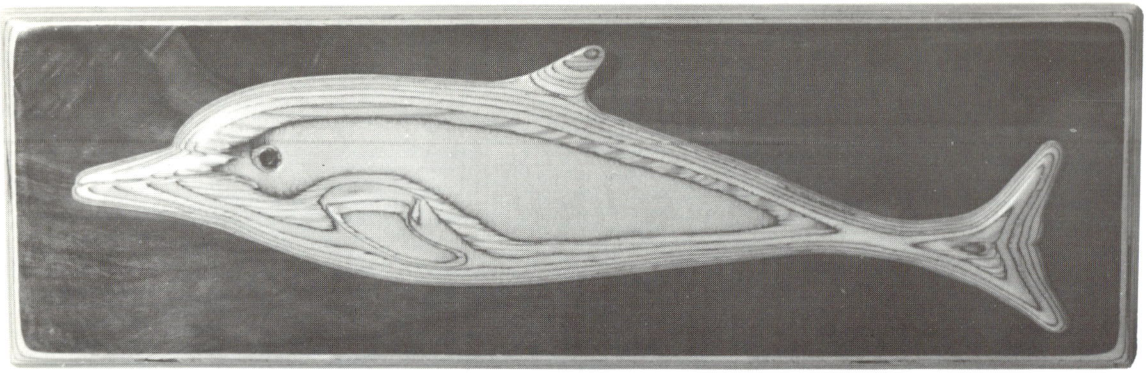

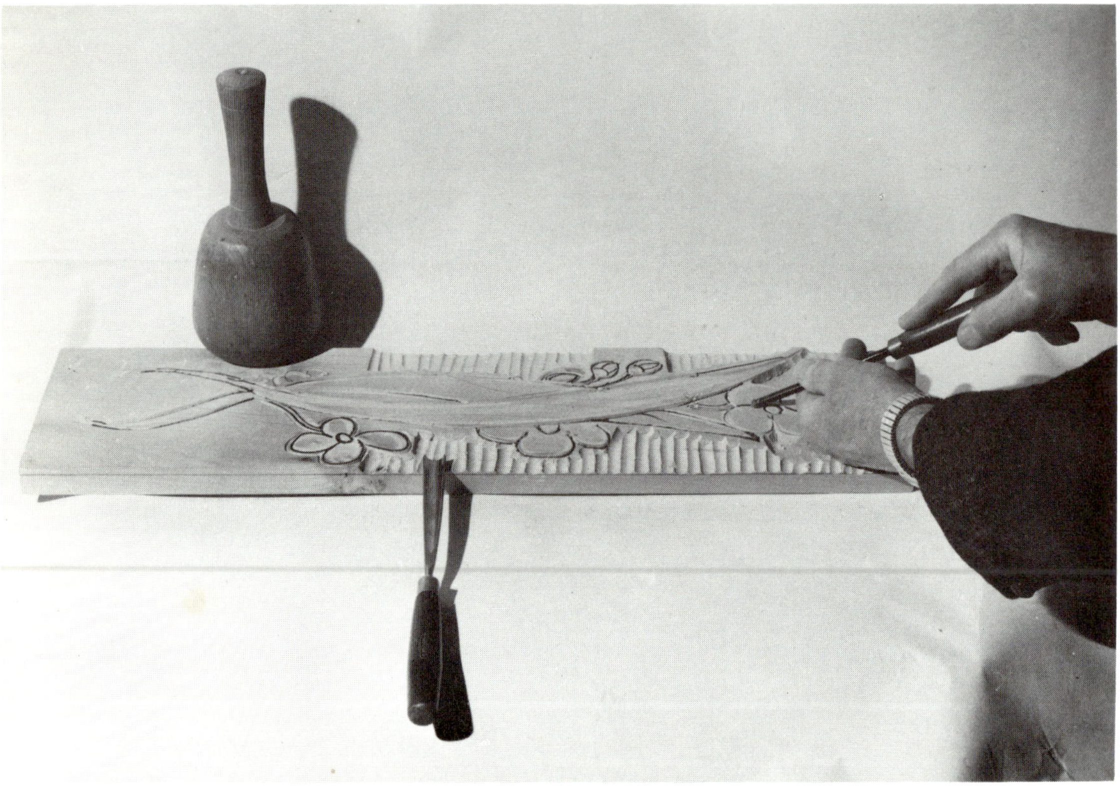

Fig. 27 (Above) Dolphin. 550mm × 175mm ($21\frac{3}{4}$in × $6\frac{7}{8}$in). A 12mm ($\frac{1}{2}$in) thick multi-ply panel faced with rosewood veneer makes an excellent background. Note the bevelled edges and rounded corners of the background. The dolphin is attached to the back panel with two screws; two small screw eyes fixed to the back enable the panel to be hung.

Fig. 28 (Below) Flower arrangement in lime. This shows clearly the marking out of the design, outlining with the Veiner gouge and removing the background with a 12mm ($\frac{1}{2}$in) No. 8 straight gouge.

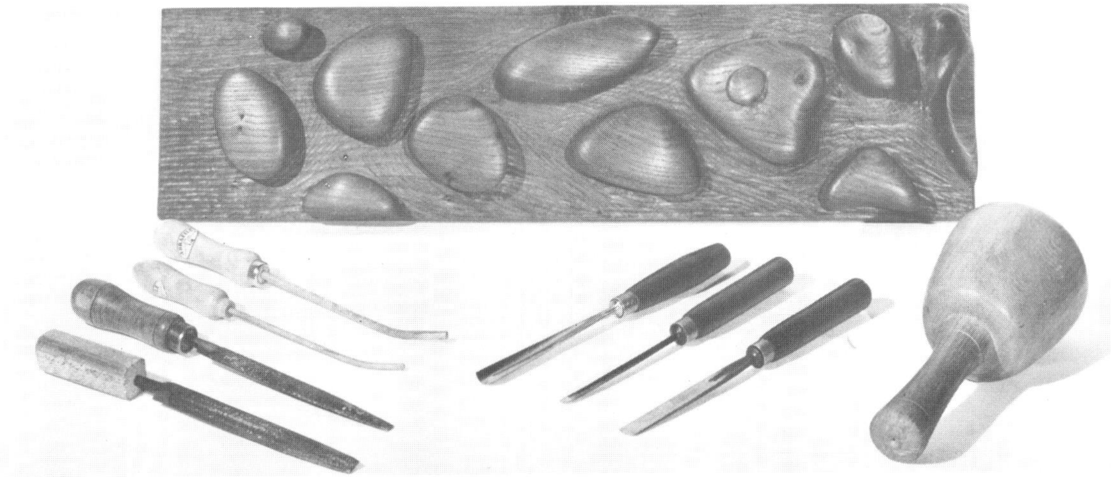

Fig. 30

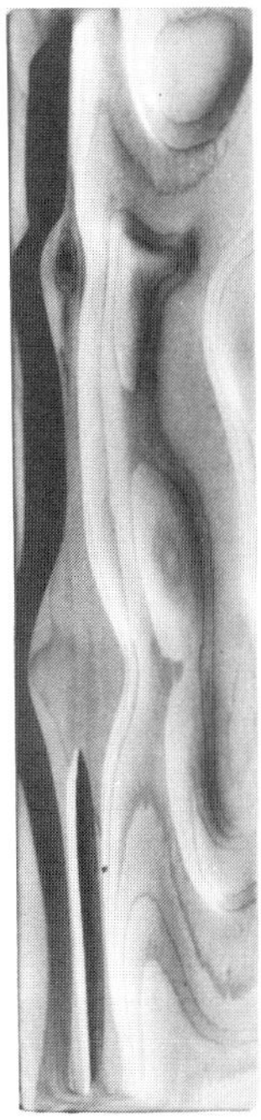

Fig. 31

Fig. 29 (Above) Falling stones. Elm, 600mm × 150mm × 35mm (23$\frac{5}{8}$in × 5$\frac{7}{8}$in × 1$\frac{3}{8}$in). The stones are smooth and well undercut in places while the background is left finished from the tool. In the foreground can be seen the various gouges, rasps and files used making this plaque. The linseed oil treatment has given warmth and depth of colour to this high-relief carving.

Fig. 30 A pleasing floral plaque in African mahogany. Made by Alfred Gorvin.

Fig. 31 Bird. Cedar, 450mm × 100mm × 25mm (17$\frac{3}{4}$in × 4in × 1in). A good example to show how grain influences design. Made by a student of Shoreditch College.

Fig. 32 Dish with leaf-carved ends. Made by Alfred Gorvin.

Fig. 32

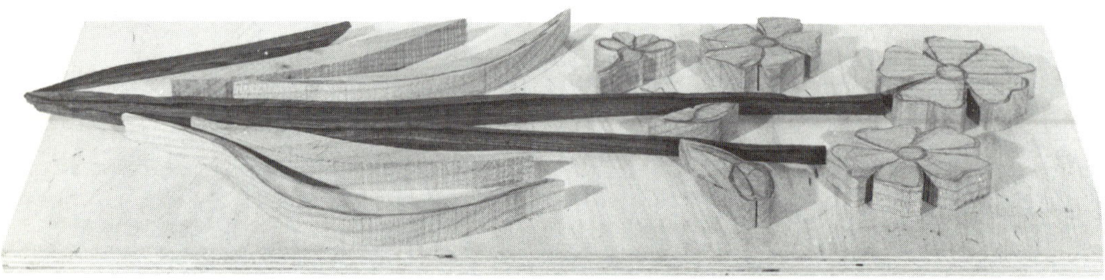

Fig. 35

Fig. 33 and 34 (Above left and right) Sketches showing ideas for floral arrangements and method of building up component pieces to form designs. The technique of using small pieces to create a design has great possibilities, is economical and can be produced with the minimum of tools. The pieces are worked separately and glued to the background. The plaques are finished with French polish or shellac.

Fig. 35 Floral arrangement in preparation consisting of rosewood for main stems with leaves and flowers in English elm.

Fig. 36

Fig. 37

Fig. 36 and 37 Floral plaques. Backgrounds are of chestnut; small pieces of mahogany, oak and yew have been used in making these designs. Made by Alfred Gorvin.

Fig. 38 (Above) Horse in sycamore. The background consists of 9mm ($\frac{3}{8}$in) plywood covered with brown hessian and lipped with sycamore. Size of frame: 430mm × 280mm (17in × 11in).

Fig. 39 (Left) Bird in elm. The grain here is prominent and enhances the design. The background consists of 12mm ($\frac{1}{2}$in) multi-plywood veneered with walnut.

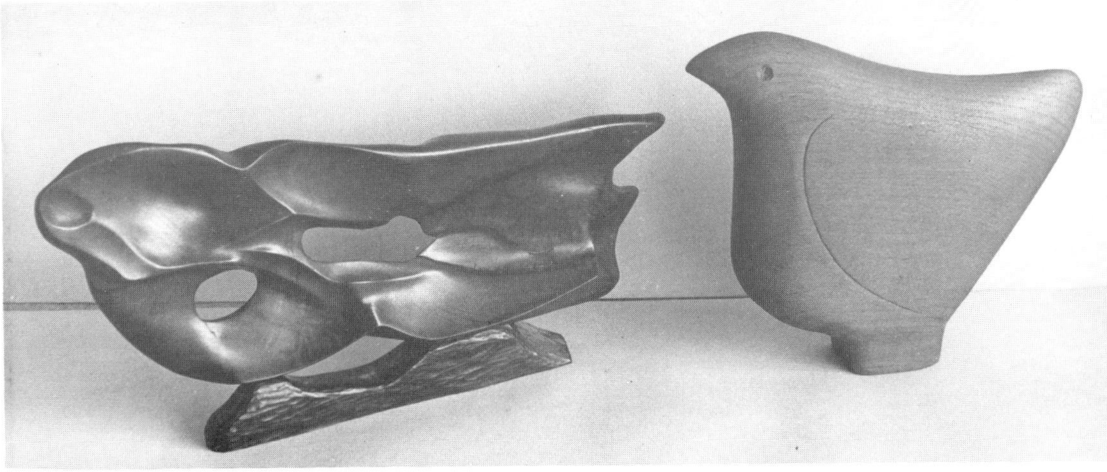

Fig. 42

Fig. 40 (Top) Two forms; that on the left is in African walnut with a rosewood base, that on the right is in teak. Made by a student of Shoreditch College.

Fig. 41 (Left) Abstract form in Scots pine, height 300mm ($11\frac{3}{4}$in). The designing and making of an abstract form such as this makes a good introduction to sculpturing wood. Working in softwood demands very sharp tools. See wood form Man, page 74.

Sculpture

Fig. 42 Fish. Plane supported by a stainless steel rod and on a utile base. Made by a student of Shoreditch College.

Fig. 43

Fig. 44

Fig. 45

Fig. 46

Fig. 43 Penguin in utile. French polish finish. Made by a student of Shoreditch College.

Fig. 44 Sail. A rather pleasant sculpture in sycamore. The sail is supported with a stainless steel rod. The teak base, left from the tool, has been cleverly arranged to simulate water. Made by a student of Shoreditch College.

Fig. 45 and **46** Further examples of Vee tool work in African mahogany. Made by Alfred Gorvin.

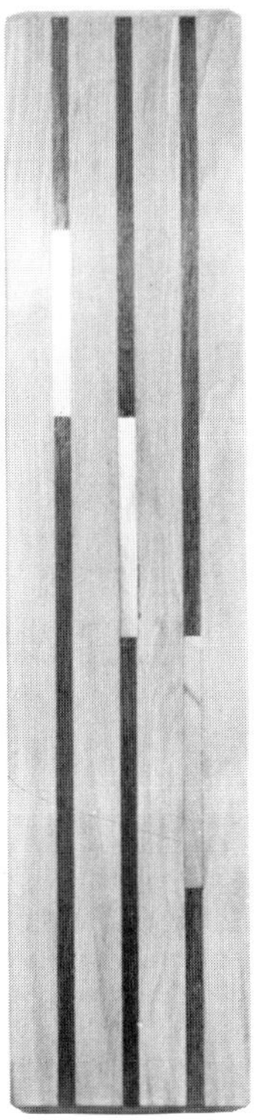

Fig. 48

Fig. 49

Fig. 47 (Above) Use of the scratch stock. Two scratch stocks with cutters and examples of mouldings they produce. The files shown were used to shape the cutters. See page 100.

Fig. 48 Plaque in Columbian pine with inlay of teak and aluminium. The grooves to accomodate the inlay can be made with a plough or a scratch stock.

Fig. 49 Plaque in utile with Greek key pattern inlaid with boxwood. 460mm × 100mm × 25mm ($18\frac{1}{8}$in × 4in × 1in). A scratch stock was used to make the majority of the grooves to receive the 'string' or 'line'. Those at right angles to the grain were cut in with a sharp knife, the waste being removed with a small chisel.

Note: 'Strings' or 'lines' are cut from about $1\frac{1}{2}$mm ($\frac{1}{16}$in) up to 3mm ($\frac{1}{8}$in) in thickness either square or rectangular in section and are about 1,000mm (39in) in length. They can be obtained in box, holly or ebony. The lines should be fitted hand-tight, glued in and pressed home with the cross-pane of a hammer. Care is needed in cleaning up; a finely-set, sharp plane is essential.

Fig. 50

Fig. 51

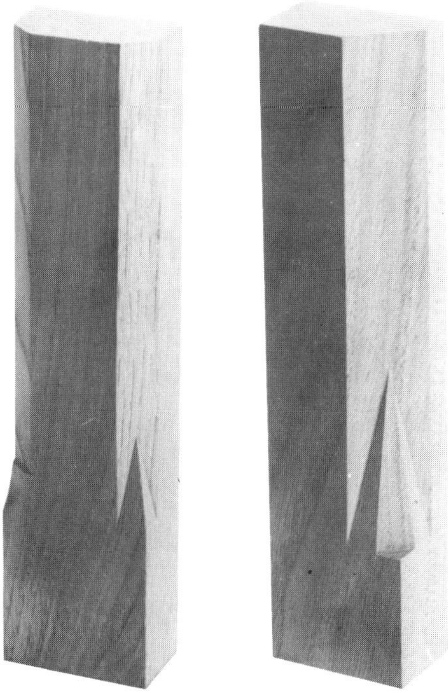

Fig. 52

Fig. 53

Opposite
Fig. 50 An exploded view of a portion of an elliptical-headed door in teak, showing mouldings worked on the solid with the scratch stock.

Fig. 51 Portion of a door in teak with mouldings worked on the solid with the scratch stock. The moulding is finished at the intersection as a mason's mitre; the panel is fielded.

This page
Fig. 52 Complex decorative stops.

Fig. 53 Example of a simple stopped chamfer.

Forms in sycamore, cherrywood and teak. Left: form in weathered sycamore mounted on a white sycamore base. Lightly French polished and waxed. Centre: form in cherrywood with yew base, lightly polished to a natural matt finish. Right: form in teak, oiled finish. The work of students at Shoreditch College.

DESIGN AND PRACTICAL EXAMPLES

The examples of work shown in this section range from designs which have been created mainly from natural forms—such as can be made from cross-cutting small trees or branches—and progressing to more advanced, three-dimensional work. Good quality plywood makes an ideal material for both small and large sculpture, the glue lines coupled with the alternating layers of veneer, which make up the plywood, giving an attractive finish when shaped. Plywood has great potential if used wisely.

Included here are many photographic examples in different woods of interesting variations of high and low relief carving, framed work and sculpture in the round. Some of the pieces are the work of students, apprentices and amateurs. The captions are designed to give further information on techniques, materials and finishes where applicable.

The designing of name plaques and the tools needed for incised lettering makes an interesting conclusion to this section.

Some design considerations for sculpture

A successful sculpture or carving must function satisfactorily in every way.

1. A well designed piece of work cannot succeed if the material in which it has been made is of inferior quality.

2. Likewise, an ill conceived design even if made in the finest material and of sound craftsmanship must be considered unsuccessful.

3. It is, therefore, important to realize that a successful piece of work must depend on good design, correct and sound material and on first class craftsmanship.

Ideas for sculpture: These can be based on the *human form,* such as: parts of the figure, a torso, a head or a hand, the complete figure, or a group of figures; or on the *animal form*—the complete figure or head, or a wide range of birds or fish, or a combination of human and animal form. See sketches of animal forms on page 50.

Fig. 1 shows the original piece of English walnut, used by the author to create the 'Dolphin' illustrated in the photographs. It is interesting to note the author's preliminary chalked outline and the natural curve of the timber. This is an example of seeing or visualising the potential and making the best use of the material for three dimensional work. The 'Dolphin' is supported with a stainless steel rod on which it can be made to turn. The base is of English elm.

Sketches for a piece of sculpture entitled 'Full Sail' are shown in photograph, Fig. 5. For the finished sculpture see page 74.

Abstract: Can be based on practically any subject matter, but it is desirable to maintain a link, although it might be remote, with the original concept. The photographs on page 66 show views of an unfinished sculpture titled 'Spinnakers'.

Realization of design

Sketching and models: It is advisable to prepare a few preliminary sketches to assist in developing an idea. Being of a three-

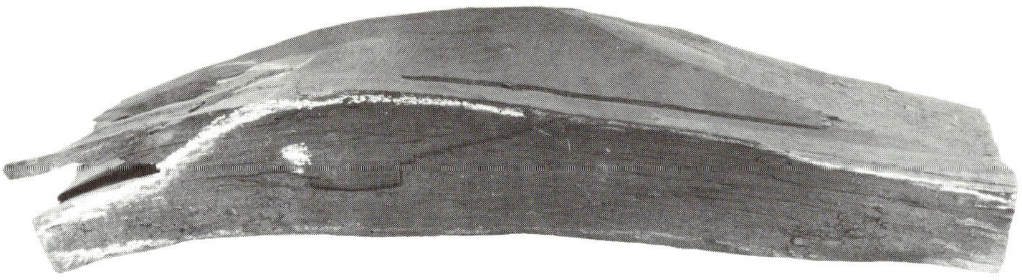

Fig. 1

Fig. 4

Fig. 2

Fig. 3

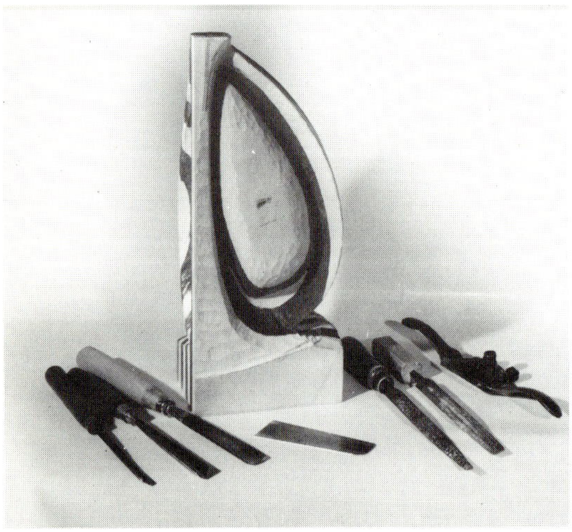

dimensional nature, sculpture is difficult to conceive on paper. A model made in clay, Plasticine or polystyrene, helps to clarify the basic idea and the general form which the sculpture is to take. Detail is not important

Fig. 1 A piece of English walnut, length 600mm (23⅝in).

Fig. 2 Dolphin. English walnut with base in English elm.

Fig. 3 Spinnakers. View showing various tools used in creating the shape.

Fig. 4 Spinnakers. Unfinished sculpture built up with 12mm (½in) laminations of mahogany and sycamore. The technique of laminating opens up many exciting possibilities in sculptural forms.

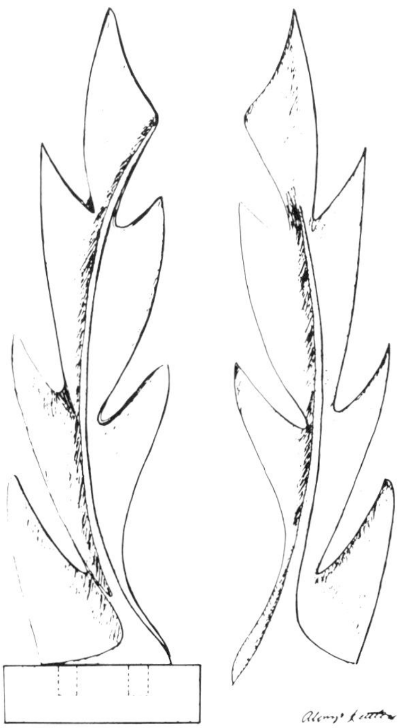

Fig. 5

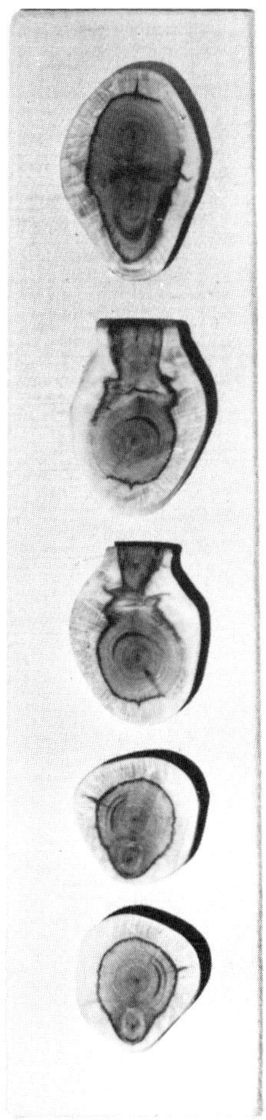

Fig. 6

at this stage, as the model is simply a guide to the general shape and proportions. See the author's note on direct carving on page 43. For relief and incised carving, see page 43.

Fig. 5 Sketches for sculpture Full Sail.

Natural forms

Fig. 6 Yew pieces cut from a small branch about 9mm ($\frac{3}{8}$in) thick glued to a background.

Fig. 7 Laburnum oyster pieces. Oyster pieces are thin slices of laburnum, walnut or yew cut at an angle of about 45 degrees from small saplings or branches. The irregular concentric rings resemble oyster shells. Used with considerable flair and skill during the seventeenth century. There is ample opportunity to develop this technique to satisfy modern requirements. Made by Gerald Reed, Glamorgan Summer School.

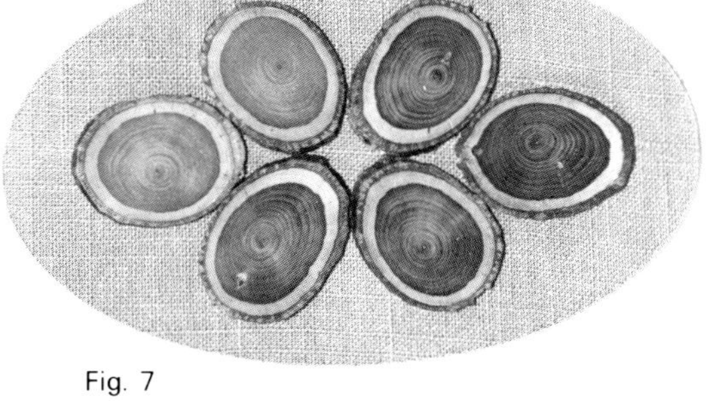

Fig. 7

Fig. 8

Fig. 10

Fig. 8 Struggle. Cut from one end of a 75mm (3in.) thick piece of yew. Very little work was done on this as the natural defects influenced and dominated the design. The base is of elm, oil finished.

Fig. 9 Natural form in yew. 700mm ($27\frac{1}{2}$in) high. Made by a student of Glamorgan Summer School. Photograph by Photography Department, Glamorgan Summer School.

Fig. 10 Tadpole. Laburnum, length 220mm ($8\frac{5}{8}$in).

Fig. 11 Seventeen. Cross section from a yew tree 150mm ($5\frac{15}{16}$in) in diameter at its widest. Overall thickness is 50mm (2in). The shape of the tree's perimeter, with its outer layers of sapwood, gives the appearance of cascading hair. The base is of brown oak, oil polished.

Fig. 9

Fig. 11

Fig. 12

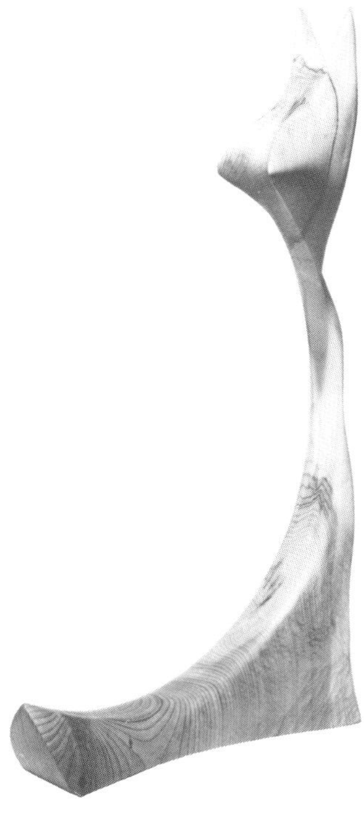

Fig. 13

Fig. 12 Predators. A curved piece of yew was cut down the centre, sculptured to shape, reversed and dowelled to a yew base. Note the grain direction.

Fig. 13 Cat form in yew.

Designs in plywood

Fig. 14 (Below) Bowl with lid built up from layers of 12mm ($\frac{1}{2}$in) plywood. The layers were practically finished before gluing up. The tool marks give a very pleasant finish. Made by Alfred Gorvin.

Fig. 15 Horse's head in plywood. Frame size 500mm × 330mm (19$\frac{3}{4}$in × 13in). Three pieces of 12mm ($\frac{1}{2}$in) plywood were glued together to build up the required thickness. The shaping to various depths brings out sharply the attractive glue lines forming delightful pattern variations. Finished with linseed oil.

Fig. 16 Owl. Height 330mm (13in). Two pieces of 12mm ($\frac{1}{2}$in) plywood were used to make this owl. The base is stained the final finish being shellac.

Fig. 17 Peacock. Made in Columbian pine multi-plywood. Various shaped irons were heated and pressed into the wood to make the attractive charred-textured surfaces.

Fig. 16

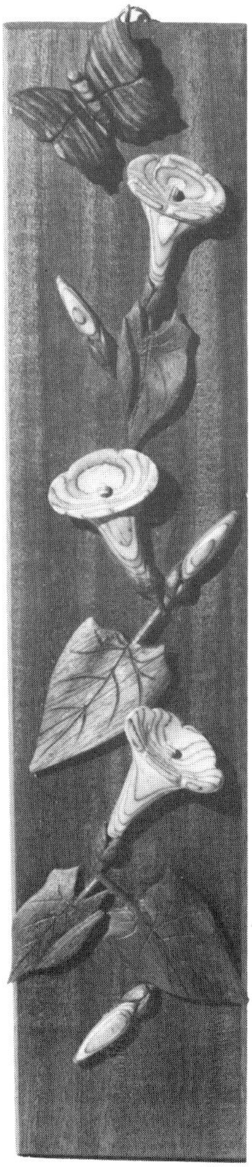

Fig. 18

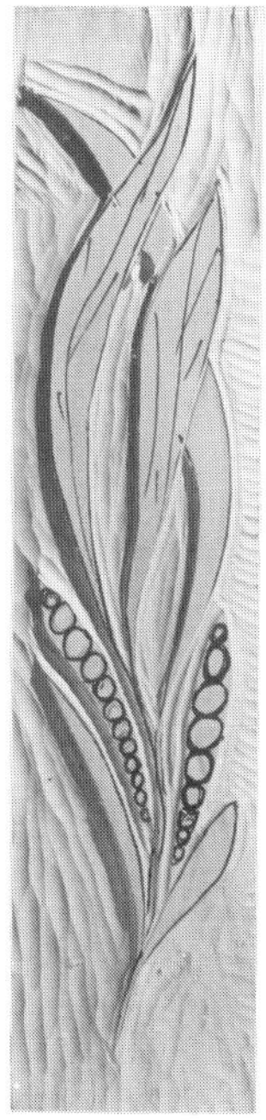

Fig. 19

Fig. 20

Fig. 21

Relief carving

Fig. 18 Convolvulus. Plywood and mahogany. Made by Alfred Gorvin.

Fig. 19 Leaves and berries. A carving in preparation.

Fig. 20 Marsh marigolds. Plywood and mahogany. The photograph illustrates the potential of plywood in this form of carving. The laminations of the veneer and glue lines, when shaped, give a realistic floral appearance. Made by Alfred Gorvin.

Fig. 21 Abstract relief in muninga. This sensitive and pleasing piece of work is attached to a framed background. Made by a student of Shoreditch College.

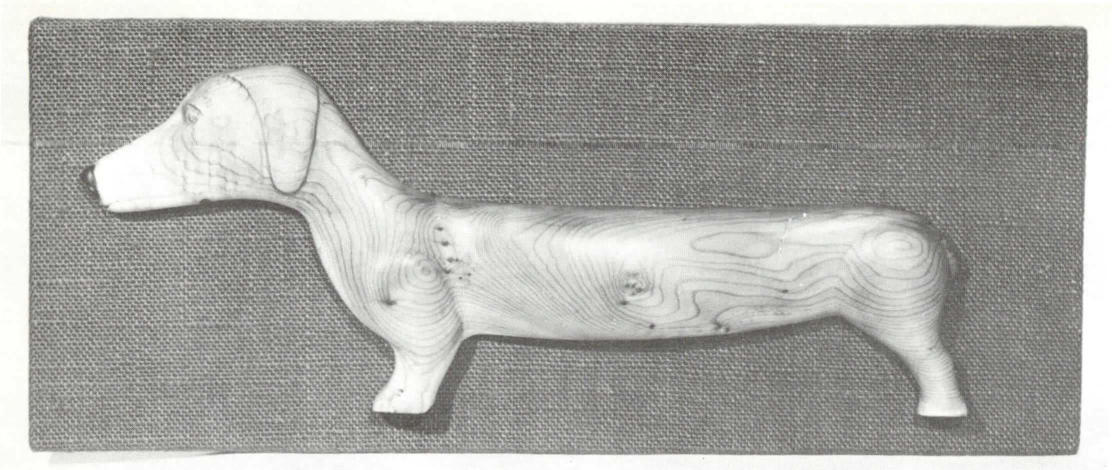

Fig. 22

Fig. 23

Fig. 24

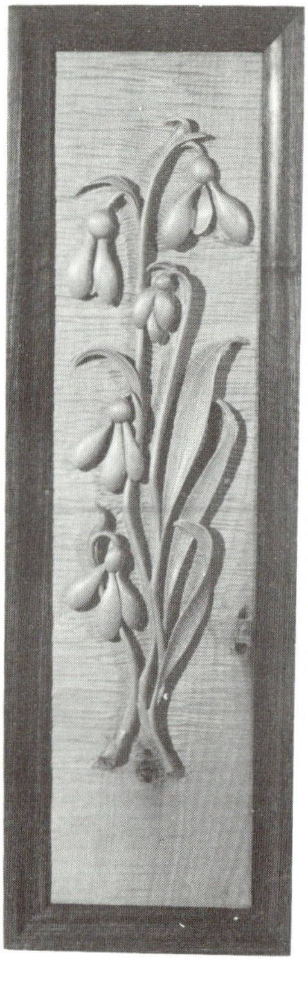

Fig. 25

Opposite
Fig. 22 (Top) Dachshund. Yew. Secured to a plywood background covered with coloured hessian. The well-marked grain gives added character to this carving.

Fig. 23 (Centre left) Impressive relief carving in cedar. The fish are mounted on a panel of rosewood-faced plywood, making a pleasant colour contrast. Made by a student of Shoreditch College.

Fig. 24 (Bottom left) Horse's head. A unique piece of yew with delightful colour contrasts of sap and mature wood. Size of frame: 380mm × 380mm (15in × 15in). Finished with linseed oil treatment.

Fig. 25 Snowdrops. In lime with a contrasting frame of blackbean. The leaves and flowers are well undercut in this attractive high relief carving. The frame, 600mm × 120mm ($23\frac{5}{8}$in × $4\frac{3}{4}$in), is jointed with mitre-faced bridle joints. See Fig. 3, page 93.

This page
Fig. 26 (Above left) Coats of Arms of the University of Ghana. Carved, painted and gilded in Heal's Decorating Studio. Photograph by courtesy of Heal & Son Ltd.

Fig. 27 (Above right) One of a pair of shields for Newbury Court House. Arms of the county of Berkshire. Photograph by courtesy of Heal & Son Ltd.

Fig. 28 (Below right) The main altar, Guildford Cathedral. Painted red and gilded. Photograph by courtesy of Heal & Son Ltd.

Fig. 31

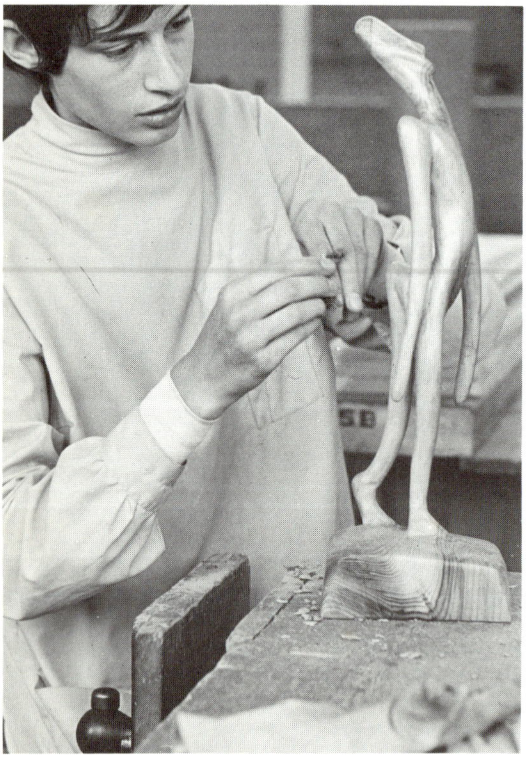

Sculptural forms

Fig. 29 Dish sculptured in rosewood.

Fig. 30 (Above left) Lamp base in cherrywood. Waxed finish.

Fig. 31 Full Sail. See Fig. 5, page 67.

Fig. 32 (Below left) Man. Scots pine. Made by a student at Glamorgan Summer School.

Fig. 33 Head form in spruce attached to a rosewood base with a stainless steel rod.

Fig. 34 Abstract form in English walnut. Made by a student of Shoreditch College.

Fig. 35 Abstract form in oak. The base has been left from the tool making a complete contrast to the form. Made by a student of Shoreditch College.

Fig. 36 Hare. Brazilian walnut mounted with a stainless steel rod on to a rosewood base. Made by a student of Shoreditch College.

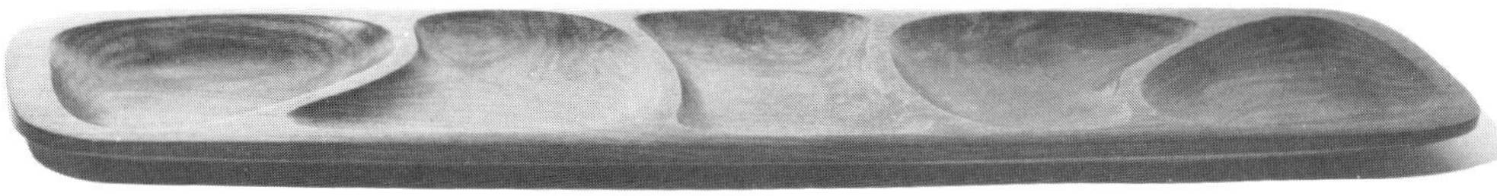

Fig. 29

Fig. 33

Fig. 35

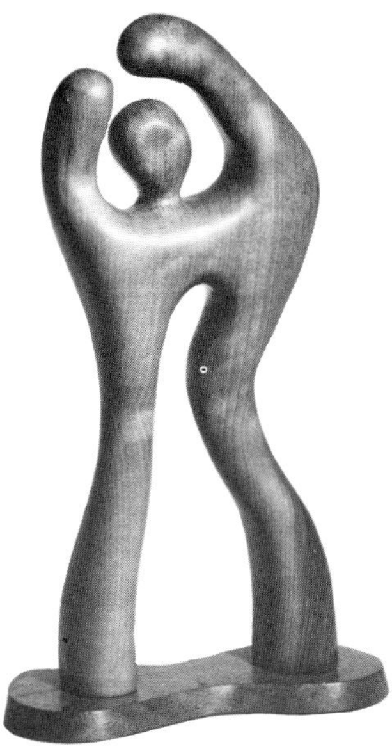

Fig. 34

Fig. 36

Fig. 39

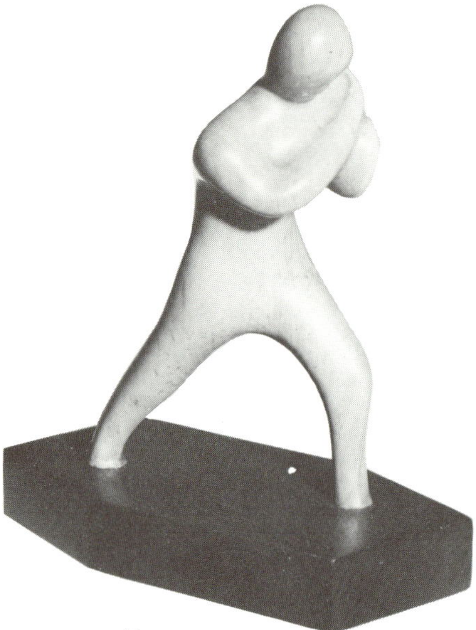
Fig. 37

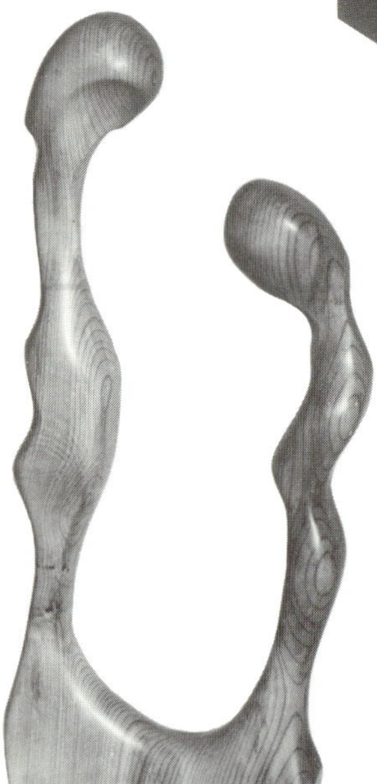
Fig. 38

Fig. 40

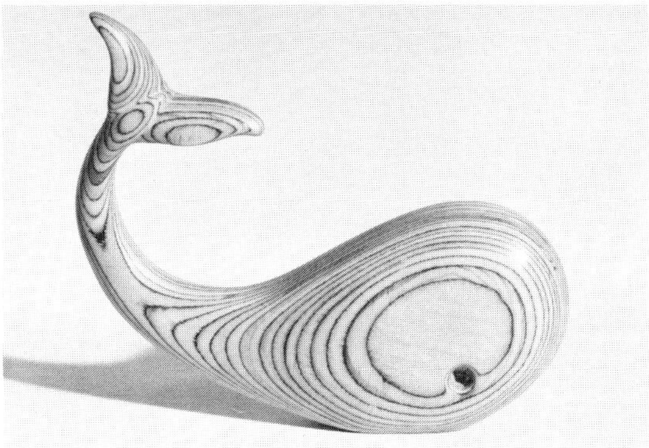

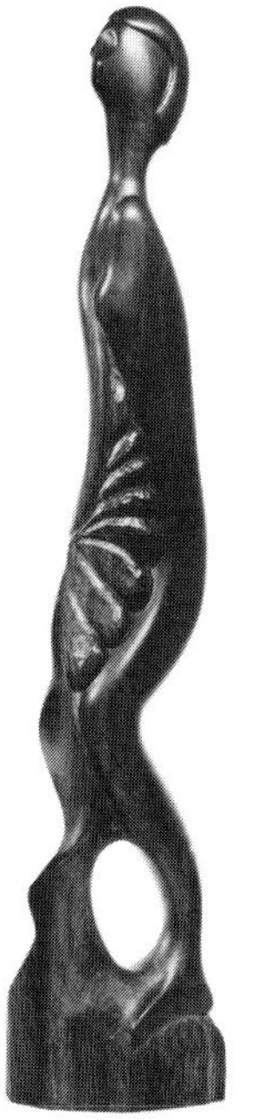

Fig. 42

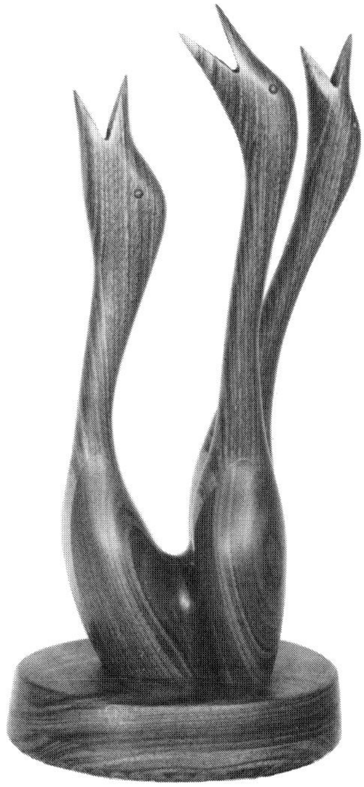

Fig. 44

Fig. 37 Action. Wood form sculptured in holly and given an oil finish. The base is sapele. Height above base 160mm ($6\frac{1}{4}$in).

Fig. 38 Together. Yew, oil finished.

Fig. 39 Abstract animal form in maranti. Length 690mm ($27\frac{1}{4}$in).

Fig. 40 Growth. Rosewood.

Fig. 41 (Above left) Whale. Sculptured in multi-ply. Four pieces of 12mm ($\frac{1}{2}$in) plywood were used to make this sculpture. Each piece was cut approximately to shape before gluing up.

Fig. 42 Fan dancer, rosewood, height 570mm ($22\frac{1}{2}$in).

Fig. 43 (Above right) Feeding time. View showing dowelling techniques for fixing finished sculpture to the base.

Fig. 44 Feeding time. English walnut, height 340mm ($13\frac{3}{8}$in). A delightful combination of colour and grain formation. The sculpture is made up of nine separate pieces of walnut carefully arranged to take advantage of the grain patterns.

Fig. 45

Fig. 47

Fig. 45 Guillemot. An attractive piece in walnut with apparent vitality. The base is of English oak.

Fig. 46 (Top) Dolphin. A satisfying piece of sculpture in English elm. The base is integral with the sculpture and not planted on. Overall length 440mm ($17\frac{1}{4}$in). Finished with one application of linseed oil, allowed to dry thoroughly and finally waxed.

Fig. 47 Bird form in English oak.

Fig. 48

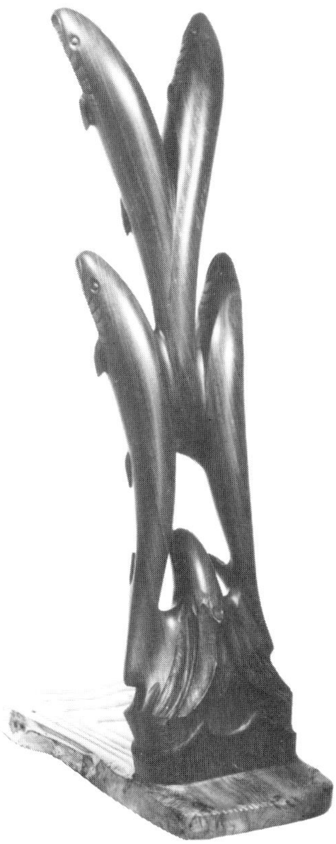

Fig. 49

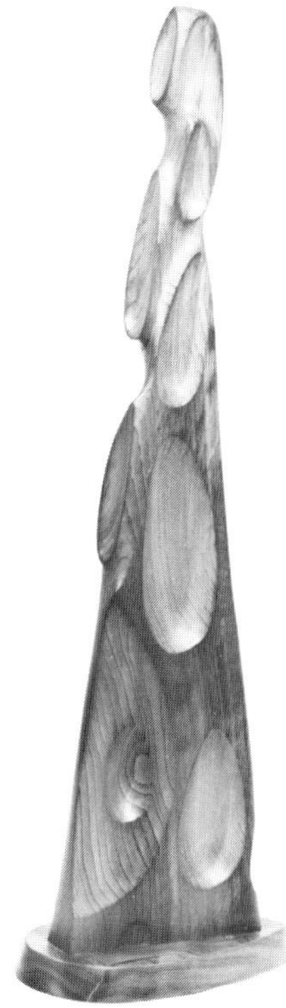

Fig. 50

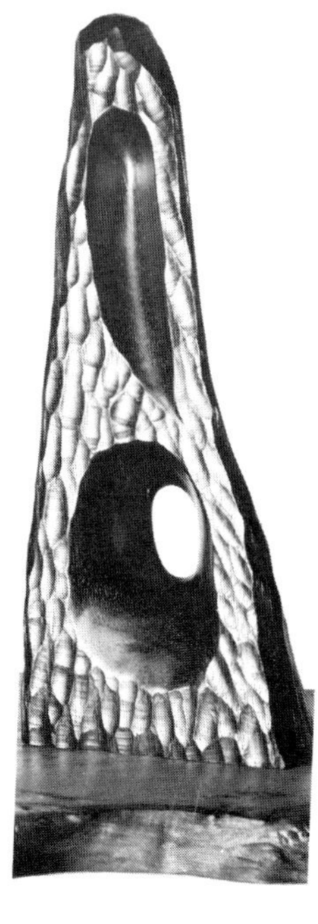

Fig. 51

Fig. 48 and **49** Salmon leap. Afrormosia, height 920mm ($36\frac{1}{4}$in). The base is in yew which has been carved to represent ripples. Finished with linseed oil, burnished and finally waxed.

Fig. 50 Raindrops. Cedar, height 940mm (37in). Base in yew dowelled to sculpture. Oil polished. See finishing techniques page 122.

Fig. 51 Abstract in rosewood. Made by a student of Glamorgan Summer School. Photograph by the Photography Department, Glamorgan Summer School.

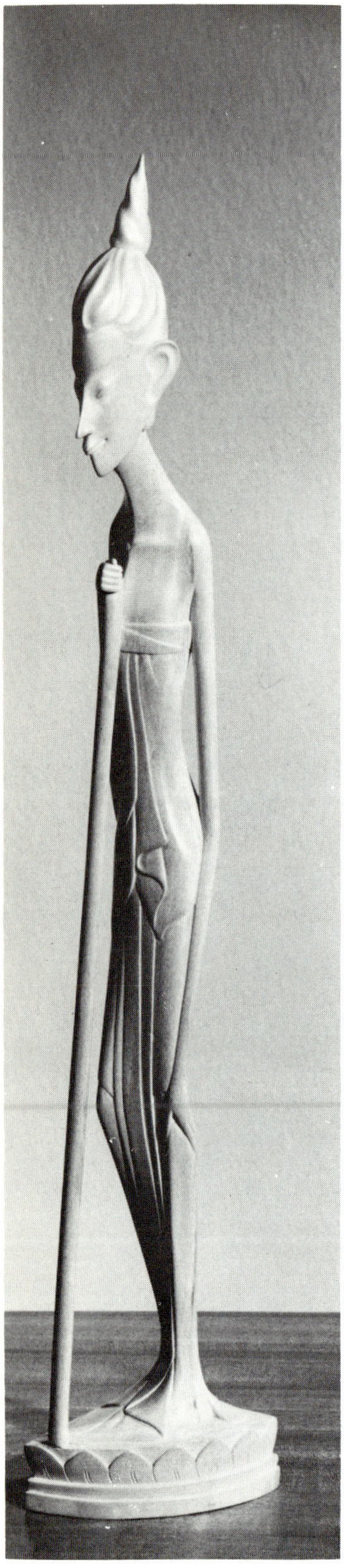

Fig. 52

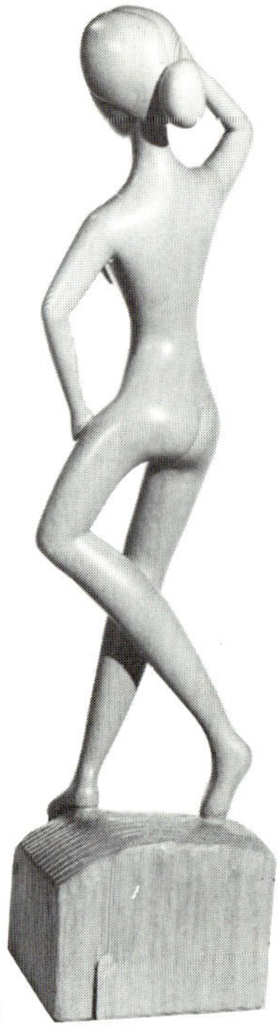

Fig. 53

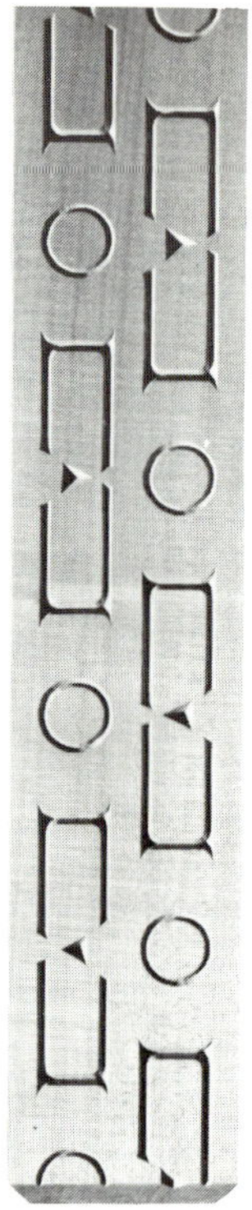

Fig. 54

Fig. 52 Morning shadow. A delightful Phillipine carving from Bali.

Fig. 53 Dancer. Columbian pine, height 610mm (24in). Shellac finish.

Incised lettering

Fig. 54 Panel of incised carving in lime. Before actually attempting incised lettering, design and make a few attractive panels. You will feel much more confident when you begin cutting name plates.

Fig. 55 Altar cross in teak.

Fig. 56 (Opp. top) Designing and cutting letters. Note the bevelled-edged chisels and selection of carving gouges to suit the curves.

Fig. 57 (Opp. centre right) Cutting serifs with a spade chisel.

Fig. 58 (Opp. bottom right) Author cutting a letter.

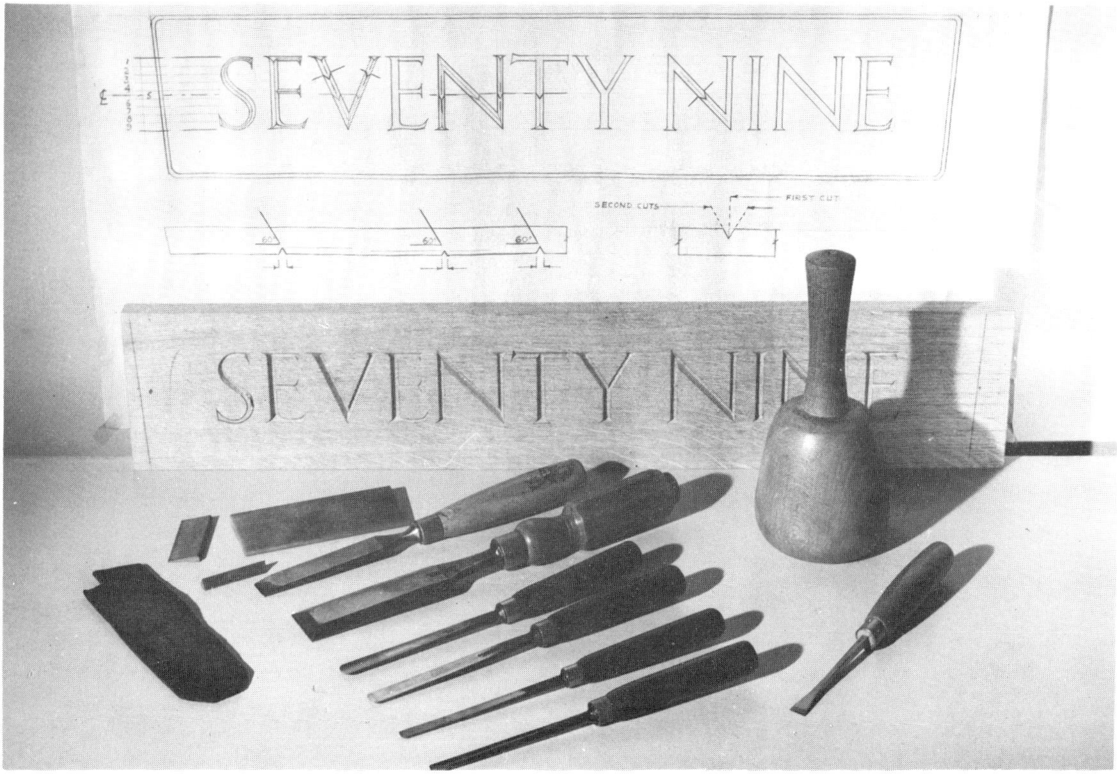

Fig. 55

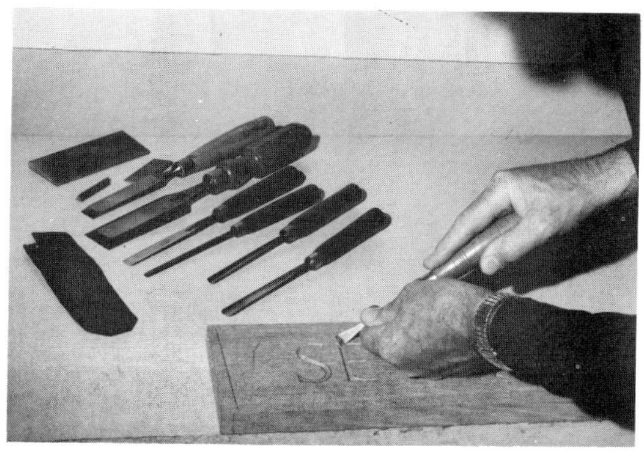

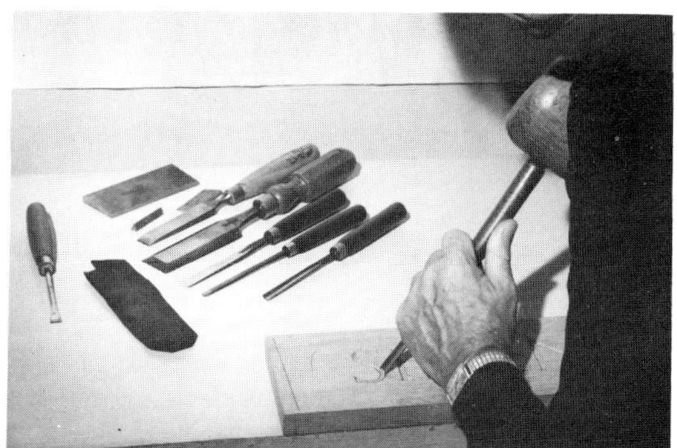

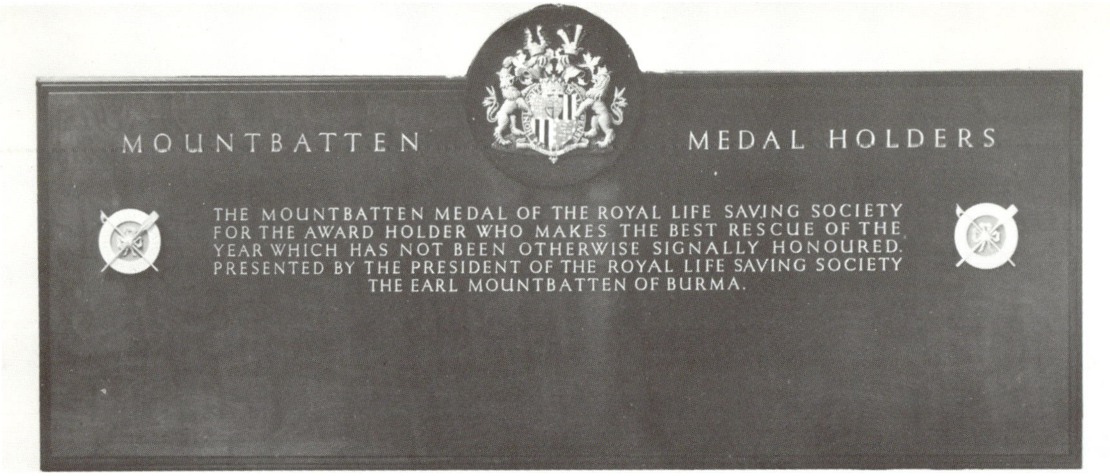

Fig. 59 (Above) Plaque. Photograph by courtesy of Heal & Son Ltd.

Fig. 60 (Below) Communion table in English oak with incised lettering on top rail.

SIMPLE VENEERING AND INLAY WORK

Veneering is the process of covering a wood—called the ground—of good quality but with poor figure, with a decorative thin wood called a veneer.

Almost every figured and exotic wood can be obtained in veneer form. Veneers are an economical method of using wood, as due to their thinness, many pieces of veneer can be produced from one log, thus making the fullest possible use of beautiful timbers.

Flat knife cut: The name of principal veneers used today. This vertical slicing method is used to produce some of the finest veneers. The timber is usually steamed before cutting, except in cases where steaming would cause discolouration. See Fig. 1.

Rotary cut: In this method the log is steamed and turned, as with a very large lathe, and the veneer is peeled off in large sheets. A large proportion of the veneers cut in this fashion are used in the manufacture of plywood. See Fig. 2.

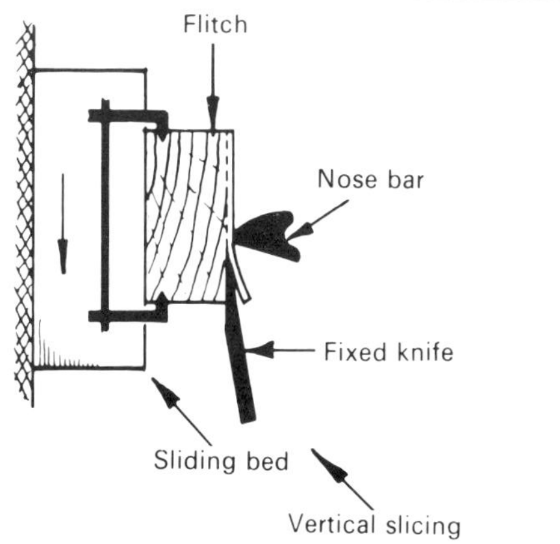

Fig. 1

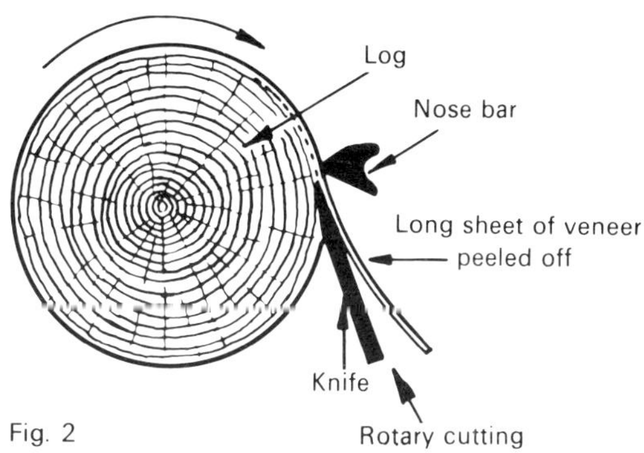

Fig. 2

Veneering

The technique of veneering by machine presses has been highly developed and a large proportion of mass-produced furniture is made of veneered chipboard.

For individual or commissioned work of a high quality, laminboard makes an excellent ground for veneering. Solid wood is also used, provided it is dry and stable and veneered on both sides. Obviously, plain non-figured material would be selected for the ground, unless for a particular reason quarter-sawn timber is specified.

Detailed information and diagrams on hand veneering can be seen on page 85.

Laying veneer by hand

There are two main methods of laying veneer by hand: with the veneering hammer, using single or double knife-cut veneer; and caul veneering, which is suitable for sawn veneer, built up patterns and veneers which are difficult to lay, or which have a tendency to cockle. A small hand-veneer press such as the kind used in bookbinding is useful. On page 86 diagrams are given for making a veneer hammer.

Procedure

For hammer veneering and the method of making a veneer joint.

1. Prepare the groundwork. Make sure it is perfectly flat. With a toothing plane, key the groundwork, planing diagonally and in opposite directions to make a good keyed surface. Usually softwoods absorb more glue than hardwoods and when laying veneers on yellow or selected pine, it is advisable to size the groundwork using a weak solution of glue, to prevent the greater part of the glue being absorbed by the softwood. Gaboon-faced laminboard, which makes an excellent groundwork for veneer, comes into this category and should be toothed and sized. Good quality multi-ply also makes an excellent groundwork for veneering. To counteract the pull of veneer, which tends to warp the ground as it dries, it is advisable to veneer both sides of the ground whenever possible.

2. Make sure everything required is ready and within reach. Fresh, hot and fairly thin glue is a necessity; tools and apparatus needed are: veneer hammer, swab, flat-iron ready heated, knife, straight edge, gummed paper strip, G cramps, sandpaper and clean hot water.

3. Arrange and match the grain of the veneer to be jointed. Mark out the centre line on the ground and identify the veneer to prevent mistakes.

4. Glue the ground as shown in Fig. 3. Lightly damp the face of the veneer with hot water to prevent it from curling when the glue is applied. The veneer must be kept as dry as possible. Excess water causes expansion and the subsequent shrinkage upon drying may induce splitting. Apply glue to the veneer, locate on the groundwork and press out the glue with the hammer. Commence at the centre and work backwards and forwards in a zigzag fashion until the air and surplus glue are forced out at the edges.

5. Test by tapping with the fingers for air pockets. If any are found, lightly damp the veneer and pass the hot flat-iron over it quickly and lightly. Keep the flat-iron clean and shiny on the sole, and always have a sheet of No. 2 sandpaper to clean it on.

6. Apply the other half of the veneer and match carefully, making allowances for the lap, Fig. 4. Joint the veneer as in Fig. 5 and 6. Locate the straight edge on the joint line, hold or cramp firmly in place. Keeping the knife close to the straight edge and with a firm and even pressure cut through the two thicknesses of veneer. It may be necessary to go over the joint again before removing the waste. Peel off top waste, Fig. 7, lift veneer and peel off inner waste. If difficulty is experienced in lifting the veneer, damp the joint and quickly warm with the flat-iron. Press the joint down with the veneering hammer, run the flat-iron down the joint and squeeze out the surplus glue, Fig. 8. To prevent the joint opening during drying, tape over with gummed paper.

7. Remove all surplus veneer and glue immediately after jointing the veneer, see Fig. 9. Use a 25mm. (1in.) or 32mm. ($1\frac{1}{4}$in.) bevelled edge chisel, let the bevel rub the edge and cut through the waste. The work must rest on a firm flat surface.

Caul veneering

The casket, illustrated in Fig. 10, combines hammer and caul veneering. The ground is prepared as for hammer veneering. Carefully cut out the veneer and build up a pattern as shown by lightly gluing the upper face of the veneer to a sheet of cartridge paper. Weight down and leave to dry. Glue the top of the lid and the veneer and locate, covering with paper. Cramp the caul, which should be heated in advance, over the veneer. The heat and pressure from the caul respectively warms the glue and forces it to the outside.

Cleaning up

Clean up edges with a plane. Use a scraper to clean off the tape and glue; never use a plane. Carefully sandpaper the surface with No. $1\frac{1}{2}$ grade, wrapped round a cork rubber. Then finish sandpapering in the direction of the grain, working through the various grades down to flour grade. Polish with white French polish, rub down with flour sandpaper or wire wool. Finish as for wax.

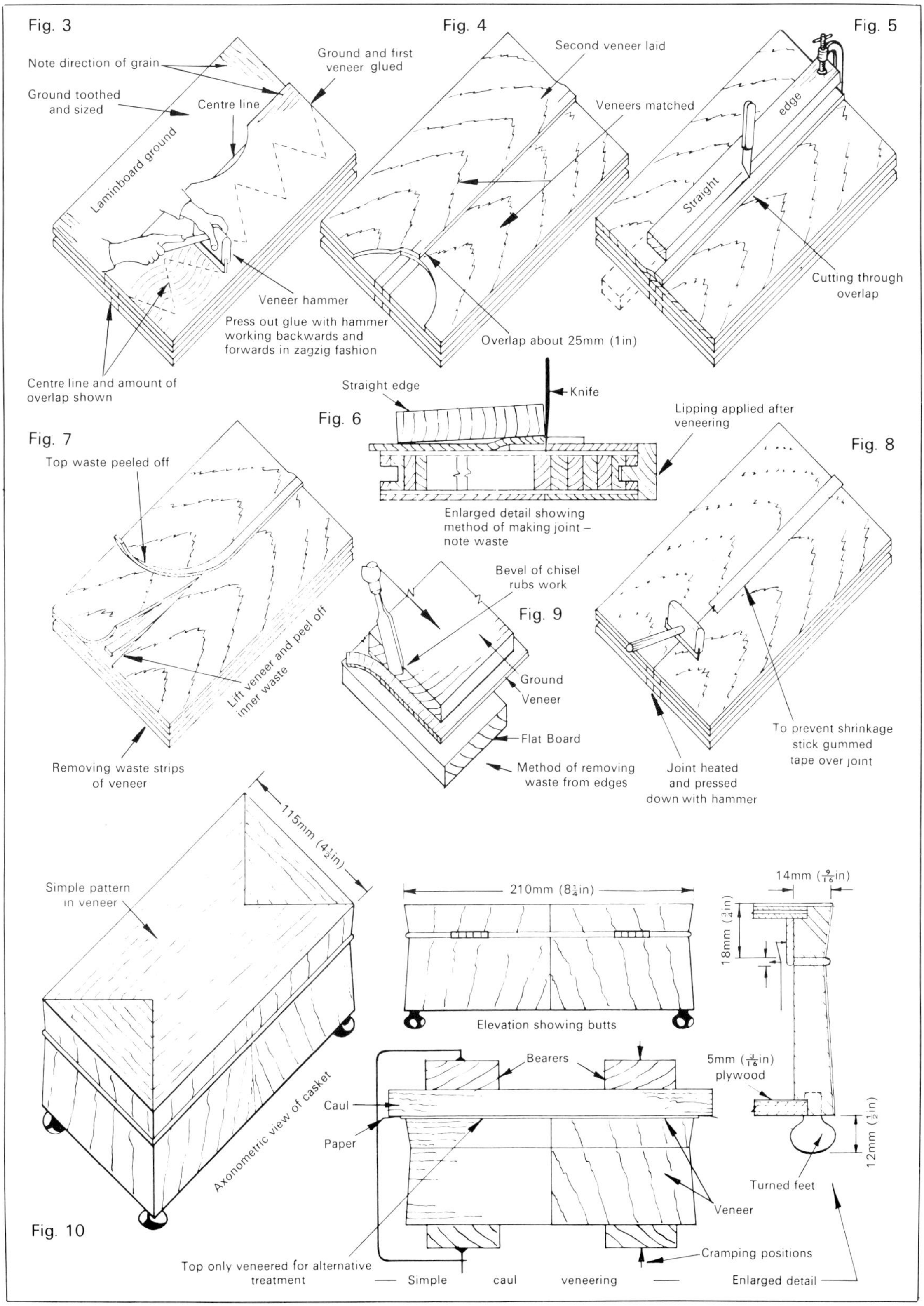

Fig. 3
Note direction of grain
Ground toothed and sized
Ground and first veneer glued
Centre line
Laminboard ground
Veneer hammer
Press out glue with hammer working backwards and forwards in zagzig fashion
Centre line and amount of overlap shown
Fig. 4
Second veneer laid
Veneers matched
Overlap about 25mm (1in)
Fig. 5
Straight edge
Cutting through overlap
Fig. 6
Straight edge
Knife
Lipping applied after veneering
Enlarged detail showing method of making joint – note waste
Fig. 7
Top waste peeled off
Lift veneer and peel off inner waste
Removing waste strips of veneer
Fig. 8
Joint heated and pressed down with hammer
To prevent shrinkage stick gummed tape over joint
Fig. 9
Bevel of chisel rubs work
Ground
Veneer
Flat Board
Method of removing waste from edges
Fig. 10
115mm (4½in)
Simple pattern in veneer
Axonometric view of casket
210mm (8¼in)
Elevation showing butts
14mm (9/16in)
18mm (¾in)
5mm (3/16in) plywood
12mm (½in)
Turned feet
Bearers
Caul
Paper
Veneer
Cramping positions
Top only veneered for alternative treatment
— Simple caul veneering —
Enlarged detail

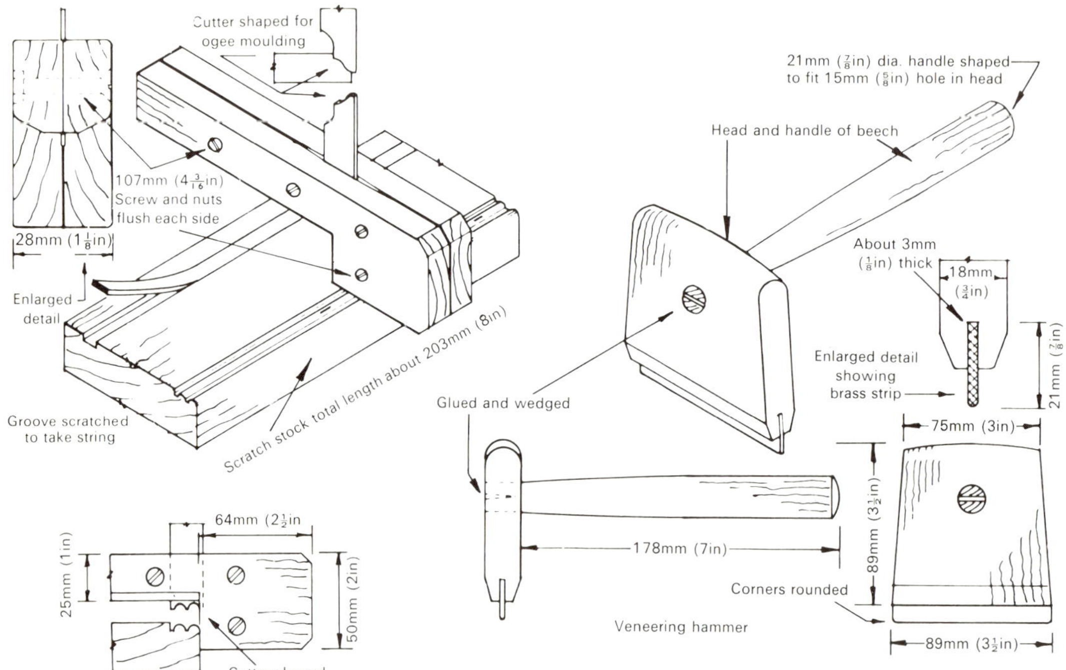

Fig. 11

Fig. 12 Backgammon board. The box is mitred secret dovetailed at the corners. The bottom and top are of 9mm (3/8in) plywood veneered with rosewood and sycamore. The pieces forming the pattern are cut accurately and taped together, the whole assembly is then glued and placed under pressure until the glue has set. Made by a student of Shoreditch College.

Inlay work

Inlaying is the art of inserting shaped pieces of thin wood or any suitable material, for example silver, brass, plastics, mother-of-pearl, or enamelled metal into a ground of wood. Refer to the section on the use of glues which also mentions inlaying.

In the section on basic designs and techniques there are a few photographs showing examples of inlay work. The diagrams on page 86 show the use of the scratch stock.

The photographs in this section cover a wide range of inlaying and veneering techniques and the captions give useful and relevant information.

Fig. 13 (Left) Three pieces of veneered work by apprentices of Heals Furniture. Photograph by courtesy of Heal and Son Ltd.

Fig. 14 (Below) Chess board and pieces made by a student of Shoreditch College.

Fig. 16

Fig. 17

Fig. 15 (Above left and right) Tantalus in rosewood veneer. This is a delightful piece of design and craftsmanship. Photograph by courtesy of Heal and Son Ltd.

Fig. 16 Casket veneered in rosewood, lippings and feet in yew.

Fig. 17 Veneered box in English walnut, with rosewood lipping, plinth and handle.

Fig. 18 (Opp. above) Yew pieces. Method of construction. The end grain pieces are cut to about 6mm ($\frac{1}{4}$in) thickness and glued to 12mm ($\frac{1}{2}$in) plywood. In the foreground are various pieces of yew and laburnum.

Fig. 19 (Opp. below) Yew pieces. Apertures inlaid with yew oyster pieces; oil-polished finish. Overall frame size: 320mm × 320mm ($12\frac{1}{2}$in × $12\frac{1}{2}$in).

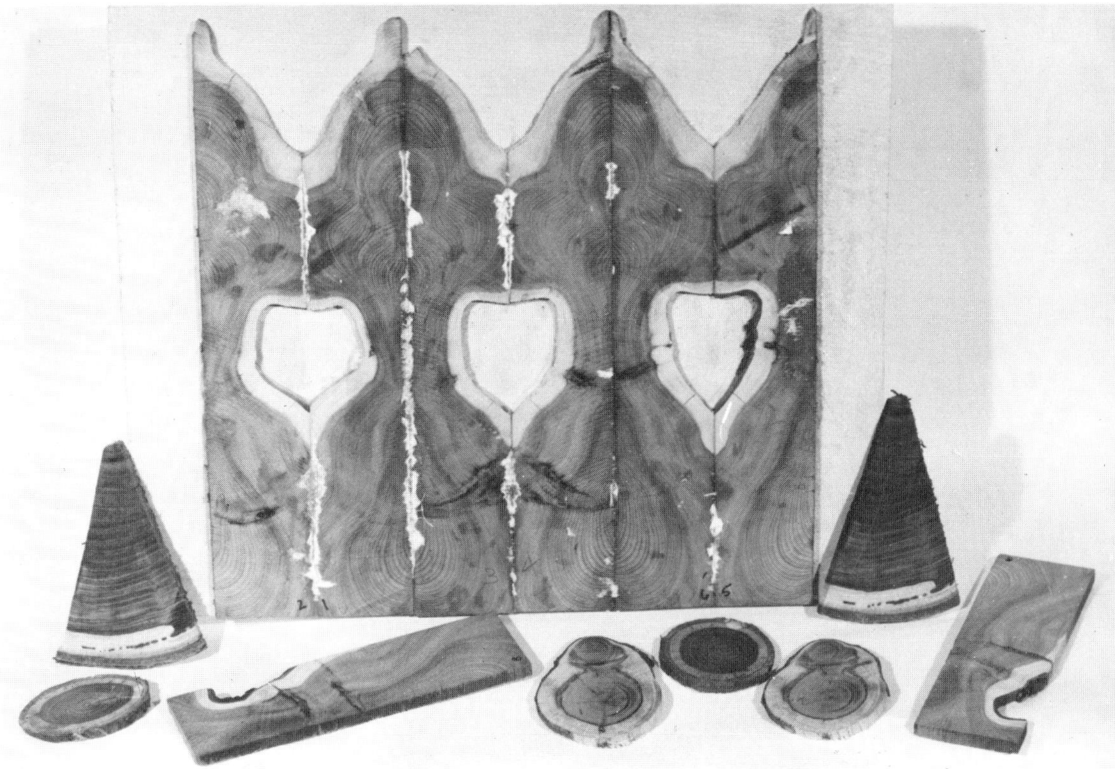

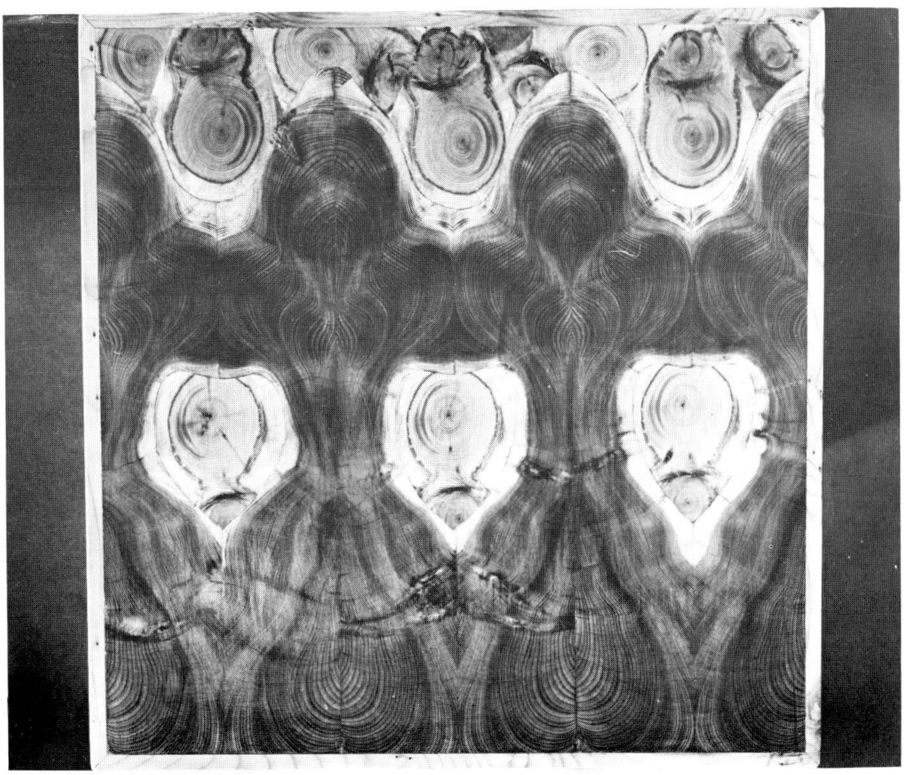

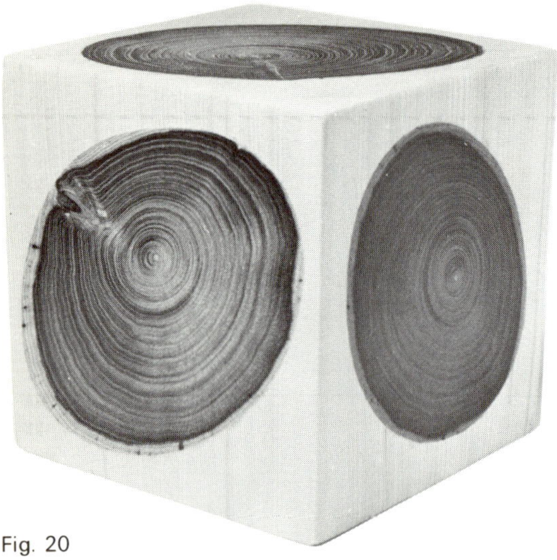

Fig. 20

Fig. 21

Fig. 22

Fig. 20 Cube of spruce inlaid with laburnum oysters. 100mm × 100mm × 100mm (4in × 4in × 4in). Photograph by the Photography Department, Glamorgan Summer School.

Fig. 21 Altar cross in teak inlaid with white Formica. See reverse side, page 81.

Fig. 22 Mahogany casket inlaid with boxwood lines.

Fig. 23 (Opp. above left) Shield in sycamore and rosewood. The insignia is in weathered sycamore veneer with a rosewood veneer background.

Fig. 24 (Opp. above right) Child's chair in oak inlaid with ebony and mother-of-pearl. Ambrose Heal, c.1902. Photograph by courtesy of Heal and Son Ltd.

Fig. 25 (Opp. below) Dining table in Brazilian rosewood inlaid with pear tree, ivory and ebony, fitted with twelve sconces set in solid silver plate. Made in the late 1950's for the Presidential Palace, Baghdad. Designed by Professor R. D. Russell, RDI FSIA. Photograph by courtesy of Gordon Russell Ltd.

DRUMMOND
ANGUS
IOAN

JOINTING OF WOOD, LAMINATING, USE OF GLUE AND EXPERIMENTAL WORK

Joints

Joints used in woodwork can themselves, when designed as such, have a pleasing decorative quality which often gives extra strength. A popular example is the through mortise-and-tenon joint as used in cabinet-making, which has been secured with wedges, usually of a different colour, for a decorative effect. Dowels with rounded ends which are arranged to project from the face of the finished work, are pleasing to the eye.

Dovetailing

Through dovetailing is a good example of the decorative possibilities of joints. A well-made through-dovetailed carcase can, by itself, be decorative and by adjusting the sizes and spacings of the pins, many interesting variations can be achieved. The illustrations show a few examples of decorative joints. Try out your design ability and skill by making a few new joints.

Jointing of wide panels for carving

Wood which is to be joined should be matched for grain and colour. In the making up of wide panels for carving, it may be necessary to join up several boards to obtain the required width. Butt joints would be quite satisfactory for joining up dry quarter-sawn timber up to approximately 25mm. (1in.) in thickness, but owing to the possibilities of movement in solid timber it would be preferable to reinforce with dowelling or loose tongues, or tongues and grooves worked in the solid. Care must be taken to position the dowels or tongues to avoid interference with the carving.

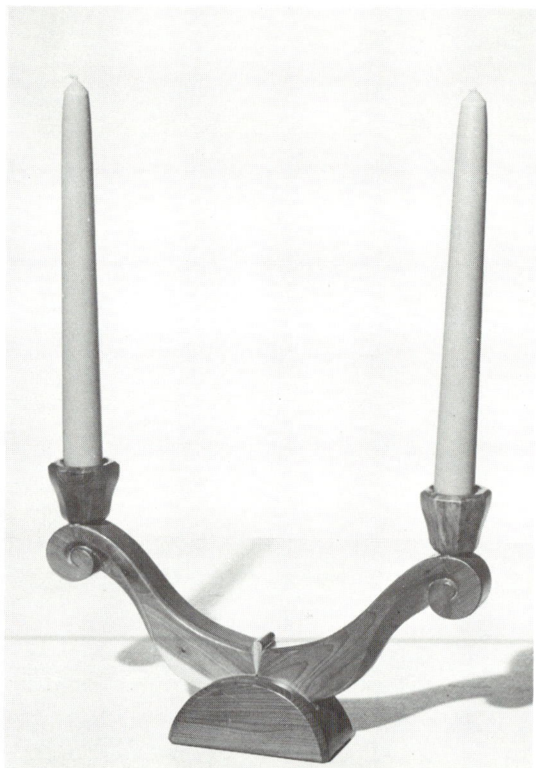

Fig. 1 One of a pair of candelabras in yew. The arms are dowelled together and the joint is decorated with a laburnum wedge, the assembly being housed into the base.

When jointing up thick slabs of wood to make a large sculpture it is advisable to keep the material not more than approximately 75mm. (3in.) thick, owing to possible movement.

Fig. 2

Fig. 3

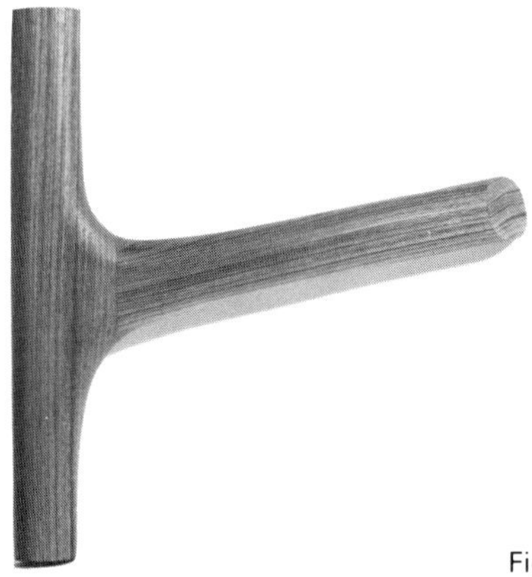

Fig. 4

Fig. 5

Fig. 2 Exploded view of mitred-faced bridle joint.

Fig. 3 Mitred-faced bridle joint with boxwood inlay. This type of joint is excellent for mirror framing and frames for panels of relief carving. See Snowdrops, Fig. 25, page 72.

Fig. 4 Sculptured joint in teak.

Fig. 5 Decorative through-dovetail joint.

Fig. 6

Fig. 7

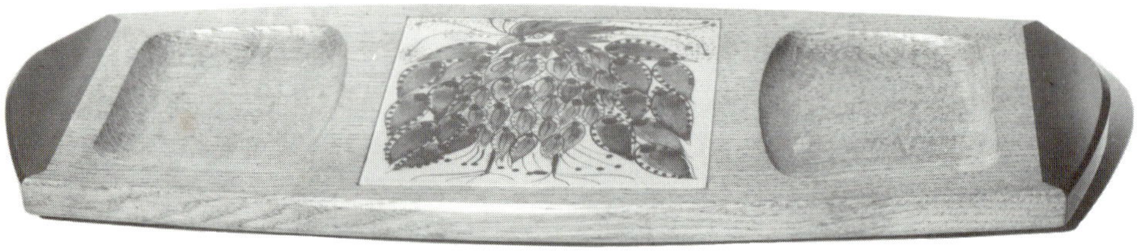

Fig. 8

Fig. 9

Fig. 6 Decorative joints in teak and oak. This saw tooth shoulder would make an attractive, as well as a strengthening, feature to table and other types of framing.

Fig. 7 Exploded view of joint. The lower rail with a through mortise-and-tenon joint is decorated with rosewood wedges.

Fig. 8 Oak tray with inset tile. The handles are of laburnum and are tongued, grooved and mitred into the tray.

Fig. 9 (Opp. below) An attractive occasional table, the decorative effect of the through-mortise-and-tenon joints is clearly visible. Photograph by courtesy of Heal and Son Ltd.

Fig. 10 (Above left) Writing bureau and book-case in oak. Main constructional features are the through mortise-and-tenon joints with decorative wedges.

Fig. 11 (Above right) Music stand in English oak. The stand is fully adjustable and is decorated with shaped feet, mouldings and decorative stops.

Laminating

The technique of laminating—gluing together thin layers of material—eliminates short grain and offers unique design possibilities, not only for shaped work in furniture and building, but also in carving and sculpture. See photographs, page 66. Forming in plywood offers similar opportunities.

Formers

Formers are designed and made to suit the required curve or shape. They are generally substantially made, mainly to hold the shape and resist pressure caused by cramping up. Formers support and hold the work to shape until the glue has set. See Fig. 19, page 103 and the diagrams showing construction of a former for table framing, Fig. 12, on page 96.

Glue

Modern glues make strong and permanent joints. Before gluing up work be thoroughly prepared and make sure you have all the necessary cramps and cramping blocks ready to hand. Try the work up dry and if satisfied

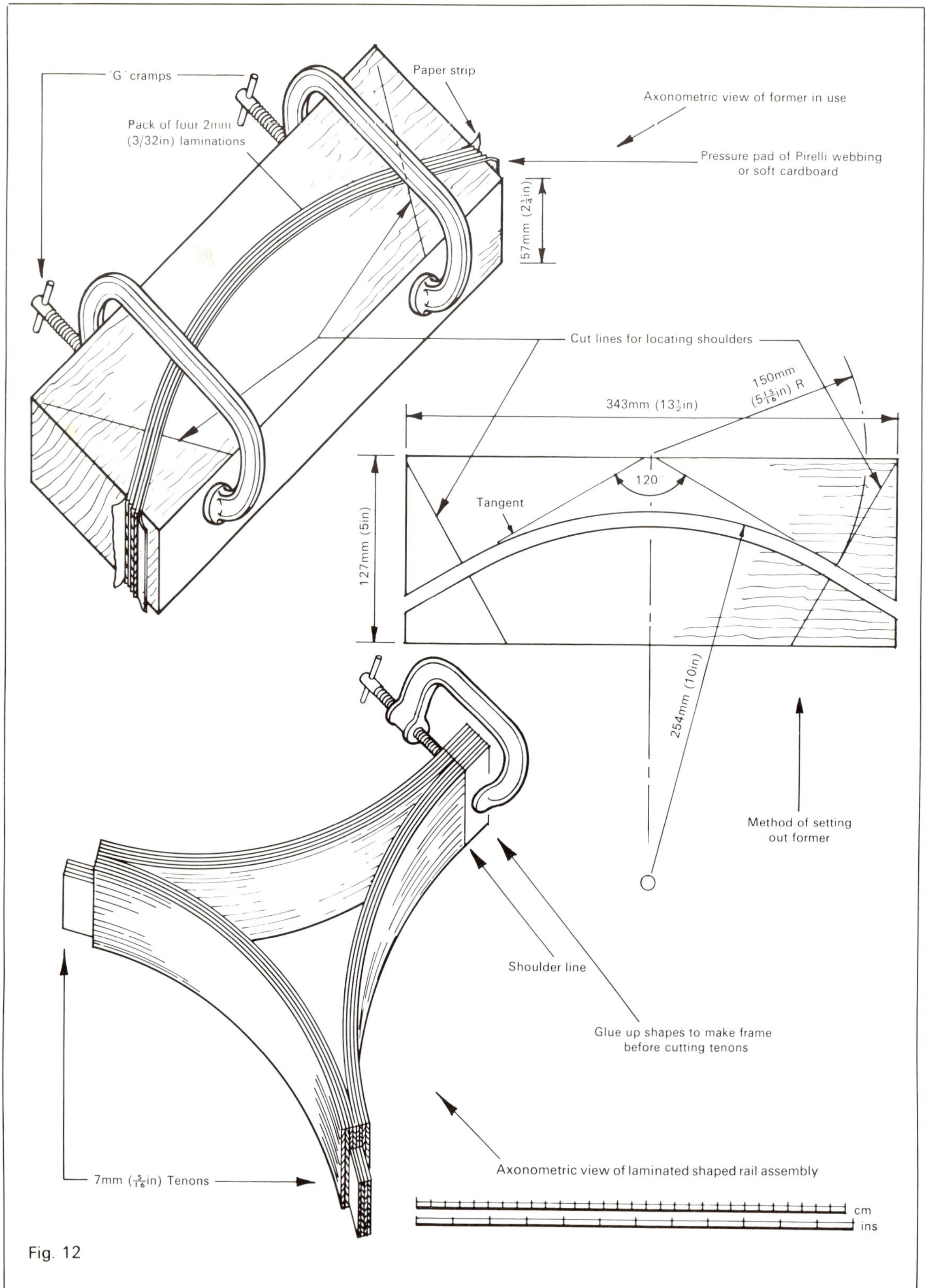

'G' cramps
Paper strip
Pack of four 2mm (3/32in) laminations
Axonometric view of former in use
Pressure pad of Pirelli webbing or soft cardboard
57mm (2¼in)
Cut lines for locating shoulders
150mm (5 15/16in) R
343mm (13½in)
120°
Tangent
127mm (5in)
254mm (10in)
Method of setting out former
Shoulder line
Glue up shapes to make frame before cutting tenons
Axonometric view of laminated shaped rail assembly
7mm (5/16in) Tenons
cm
ins

Fig. 12

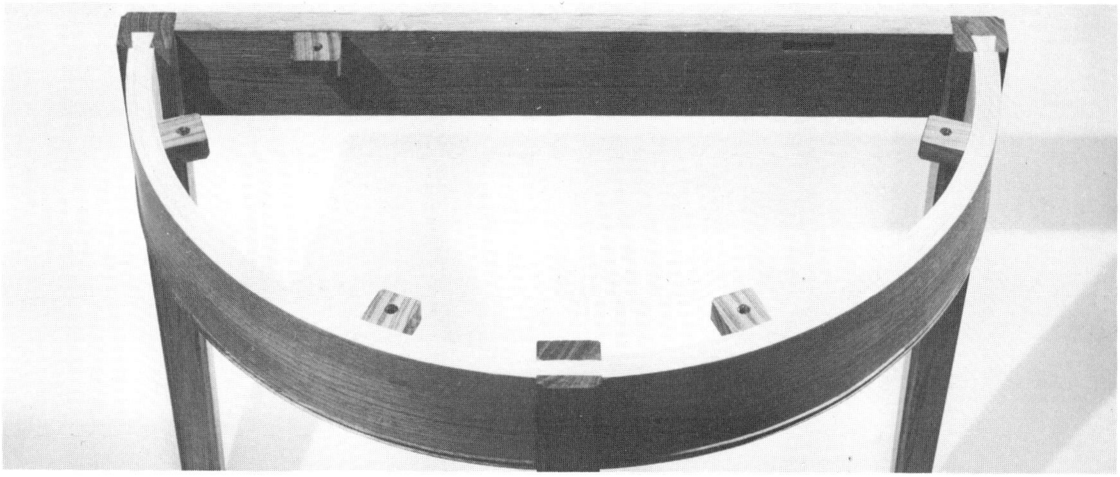

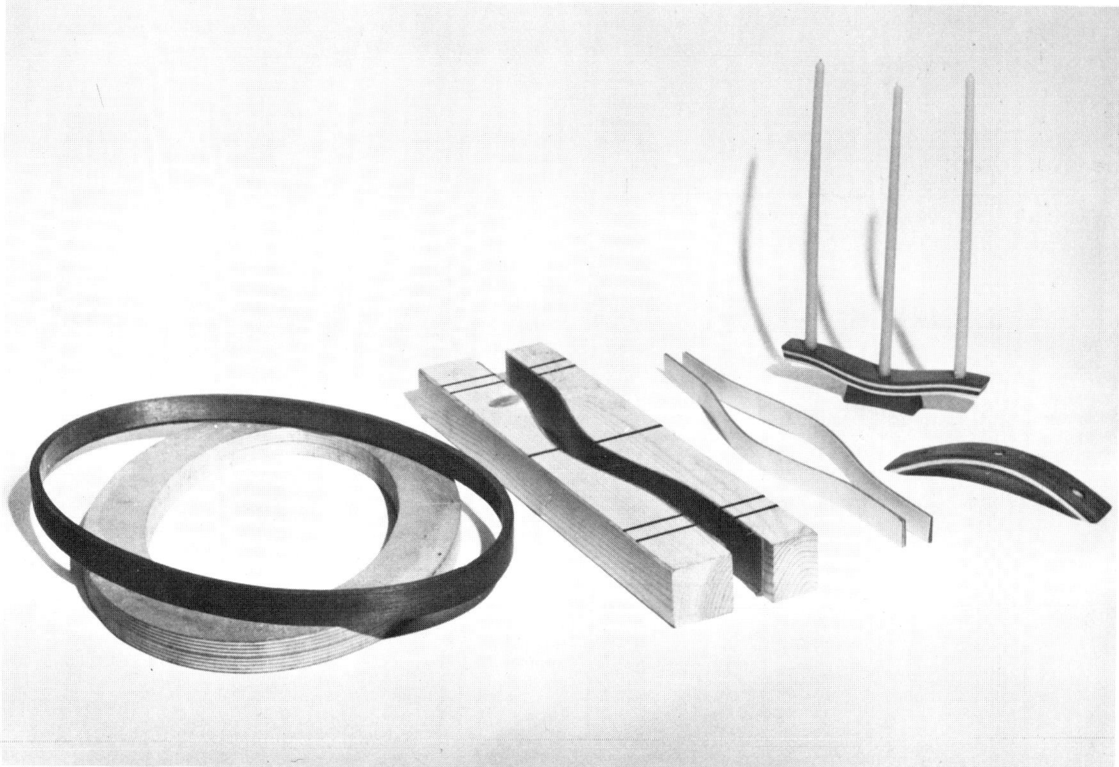

Laminated and shaped work

Fig. 13 (Above) Semi-circular table with laminated beech rim. The rim is dovetailed housed into the rear legs and the front leg is bridle jointed to the rim. All the legs are decorated with cavetto mouldings.

Fig. 14 (Below) Formers for laminated elliptical trays and other miscellaneous articles.

with the accuracy, proceed with the gluing up. A large range of glues is manufactured, but those most suitable for our purposes come under two main categories: animal and synthetic.

Animal glues

Scotch glue which is made from the skins and bones of animals is the best known animal glue. This glue is marketed in slab and in bead form (pearl glue). Care is needed in preparing Scotch glue, the slab should be broken up, covered with water and left overnight to soak. The glue jelly should be heated in a glue pot having a double container to prevent overheating and burning. Overheating destroys the adhesive properties of this glue which must be used hot and with a consistency not too thick i.e. it should run freely off the brush. For best results it is advisable to work in a warm, draught-free workshop.

Scotch glue is excellent for rubbed joints, for gluing up furniture such as chairs and stools and for veneering. Generally it is a cheap, versatile glue, and has the advantage of being light in colour and so not liable to stain the glue line.

Croid glue: Another form of animal glue. It is obtainable in tins for either hot or cold use.
Advantages: Animal glues do not dull the cutting edges of tools to the same extent as synthetic glues during the cleaning up processes.
Disadvantages: Animal glues should be used neither for external work, nor in damp situations, nor where there is a possibility of prolonged heating.
Casein glue: Further form of animal glue, the main constituent being skimmed milk. It is very strong and can be used cold. It is more water resistant than other animal glues. All joints require cramping. This glue tends to discolour the glue line.

Synthetic glues

Two well known makes of resin glue are Aerolite and Cascamite. These and similar modern glues have influenced design, construction and production over the whole of the woodworking industry. They are widely

Fig. 15 Framed mounting for an antique pot lid. Elliptical centre moulding is built up of laminated mahogany.

used in the manufacture of laminated structures for building (timber engineering), in the moulding and shaping of component parts for furniture and in the making of waterproof plywood for the boatbuilding industry.

Preparation: The glue must be used strictly in accordance with the manufacturer's instructions.
Aerolite: Can be purchased in various grades to suit specific requirements. For home or workshop use, Aerolite 306, which consists of a powder and a separate hardener, is simple to use. The powder is mixed with water to make the resin liquid. This is applied to one part of the joint and when it makes contact with the hardener or accelerator, which is applied to the other part of the joint, a chemical action is set up which sets the resin rock hard. The resin liquid can be applied with a clean brush, a wooden spatula or rubber roller. The hardener can be applied with a clean brush which must be free from metal fittings, or with a stick which has a felt pad tied to it.

Fig. 16 Shaped furniture with laminated rails. Photograph by courtesy of Heal and Son Ltd.

Cascamite 'One Shot': The resin and hardener are incorporated in powder form and the glue is ready for use when mixed with the correct quantity of water. The glue is applied to both parts of the joint with a wood spatula or roller. Care is needed when mixing quantities as any remaining glue will harden and be wasted.

Advantages: Resin glues are extremely strong, unaffected by moisture and completely resistant to attacks by mould and insects. A longer period for assembly is available and the setting time can be extended according to the type of hardener used.

Disadvantages: Any surplus glue dries rock hard and is difficult to remove. It tends also to dull edge tools when cleaning up.

P.V.A. (Polyvinyl acetate): Glue based on vinyl resins. P.V.A. glues are the latest development in the range of synthetic adhesives. They are very versatile and can be used to glue such materials as wood, hardboard, tiles, plastics, and fabrics.

Preparation: No preparation is required as they are applied to the work direct from the container. They are white in colour and non-staining. P.V.A. glues have an indefinite storage life if kept away from freezing conditions, though they should be stirred occasionally. They can be applied with a spatula or a brush. These glues are not waterproof or suitable for high temperatures or humidities.

Contact or Impact adhesives: These glues are of the rubber-latex type and are comparatively simple to use. Adhesion takes place immediately the joint surfaces touch. Ideal for such bonding as Formica laminates to multi-ply or laminboard in the making of table tops, dinner waggons, working surfaces, and trays.

N.B. It is most important to select the correct glue to suit the environment and function of the piece of work.

Interior work: Animal or P.V.A. adhesives. In a damp-free area, otherwise use an exterior grade of adhesive.

Linenfold panel.

Opposite
Linenfold panel made by the author for the Worshipful Company of Carpenters 1958 Craft Competition. The task set for this competition was a linenfold panel with shaped and recessed ends, the frame having a double-reeded moulding worked on the solid with solid worked stops at the bottom finishing on a bevelled edge and intersecting to corners finished as Bishop's mitres. The job was required to be made by hand and finished left from the tool.

Exterior work: Use synthetic adhesives. Painting gives protection and can increase the life of some glues. There are many types of adhesives suitable for various exterior conditions and it is recommended that the craftsman consult the advice given by the manufacturers.

Adhesives for special uses

Brass inlay: Use Araldite epoxy resin. An alternative is Scotch glue with a little plaster of Paris added, or one pint of Scotch glue with a tablespoonful of Venice turpentine. A little garlic added to Scotch glue keeps it fresh, increases its strength and makes it particularly useful for gluing metal inlays.

Ivory and Celluloid: Coat the inlay with a paste made from celluloid dissolved in ether, then proceed as with Scotch glue.

Tortoiseshell: Preferably use synthetic resin or Salisbury glue.
Baize and leather: Bookbinders' or table lining paste, or thin hide glue.
Plastics to wood: Cascamite One Shot, used with pressure. Impact adhesive.
Hessian and other fabrics: Copydex, a rubber based fabric adhesive—gives a good bond and remains flexible.

Fig. 17

Opposite
Fig. 17 (Above) Jewel casket in yew. The front ends and top are all shaped. The casket is mitred secret-dovetailed jointed.

Fig. 18 (Below) Communion rail in oak for Egham Parish Church. Made by students of Shoreditch College.

This page
Fig. 19 Formers and examples of laminated work. Made by students of Shoreditch College.

TURNING

This section has been planned to incorporate good design and show a wide range of turning techniques. One of the first essentials of any craft in wood is to learn the techniques of grinding and sharpening. Without sharp tools, whether gouges or scrapers, good work cannot be produced. This is particularly true in relation to turning.

The diagrams show various turning techniques and the captioned photographs give information on design features and materials. The designs include: spindle or centre turning, where the grain of wood is parallel to axis of rotation and faceplate turning, where the grain of the wood is at right angles to the axis of rotation.

The top row in Fig. 1 shows tool forms for spindle turning. It is important that a single bevel is maintained. Grinding should be done on a whetstone as the edge angle is too thin for a dry emery wheel to be used without serious risk of overheating the steel and 'drawing the temper'. The final edge is obtained by honing with an oilslip, taking care to maintain the single bevel.

The tool forms for faceplate turning are shown in Fig. 1, the lower row. For gouges a single bevel is essential. The thick bevel and quick curvature of the gouge makes it possible with 'light grinding' to sharpen direct from an emery wheel without burning the edge. With fine grained woods a honed edge may improve the finish. For scraping tools, frequent sharpening is necessary and the second bevel saves time and reduces the risk of overheating. A honed edge, possibly turned up with a burnisher, may improve the finish with some woods. Thus, Fig. 1 shows tool forms for centre and faceplate turning and particulars of scraper tools.

Fig. 2 illustrates centre turning for spindle work. The diagrams Fig. 2A-D show the method of turning tool handles, Fig. 2E gives the making of decorative V cuts and Fig. 2F illustrates the drilling of a hole for a tang. The use of the scraper tool for shaping a handle is given in Fig. 2G. Note the direction of the cut and the angle of the tool.

The centreing of material for spindle work is given in Fig. 3. These diagrams show how the long boring tool is used on table lamps. See the inlay work on the table lamp column in Fig. 3,1.

The method of turning a bowl is shown in Fig. 4. This method is particularly suitable for use in schools and colleges and dispenses with the necessity of gluing the bowl disc to a softwood mounting block. As it is sometimes necessary to remove the bowl before completion, this method is useful as the bowl can be accurately re-centred.

Where it is not permissible to have screws in the base of a bowl, the bowl disc may be glued to a softwood block to which the faceplate is screwed, or the base of the bowl could be designed to have a projection spigot which could be glued into a hole of similar size made in a softwood block. Remember to place paper between jointing surfaces when gluing a bowl blank to the block, so the finished bowl can be easily removed.

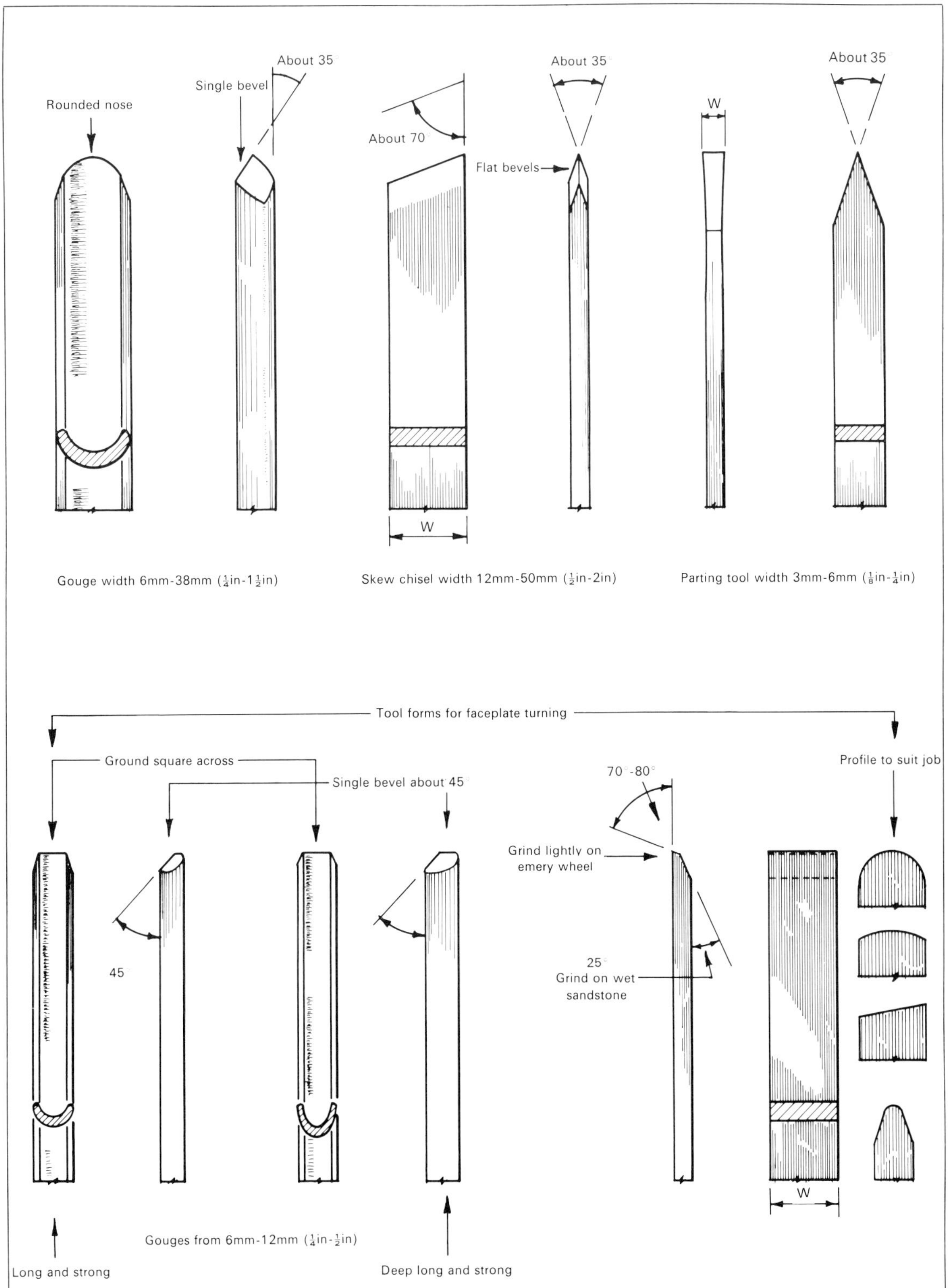
Rounded nose
Single bevel
About 35°
About 70°
W
About 35°
Flat bevels
W
About 35°
Gouge width 6mm-38mm (¼in-1½in)
Skew chisel width 12mm-50mm (½in-2in)
Parting tool width 3mm-6mm (⅛in-¼in)
Tool forms for faceplate turning
Ground square across
Single bevel about 45°
45°
70°-80°
Grind lightly on emery wheel
25°
Grind on wet sandstone
Profile to suit job
W
Long and strong
Gouges from 6mm-12mm (¼in-½in)
Deep long and strong

Fig. 1

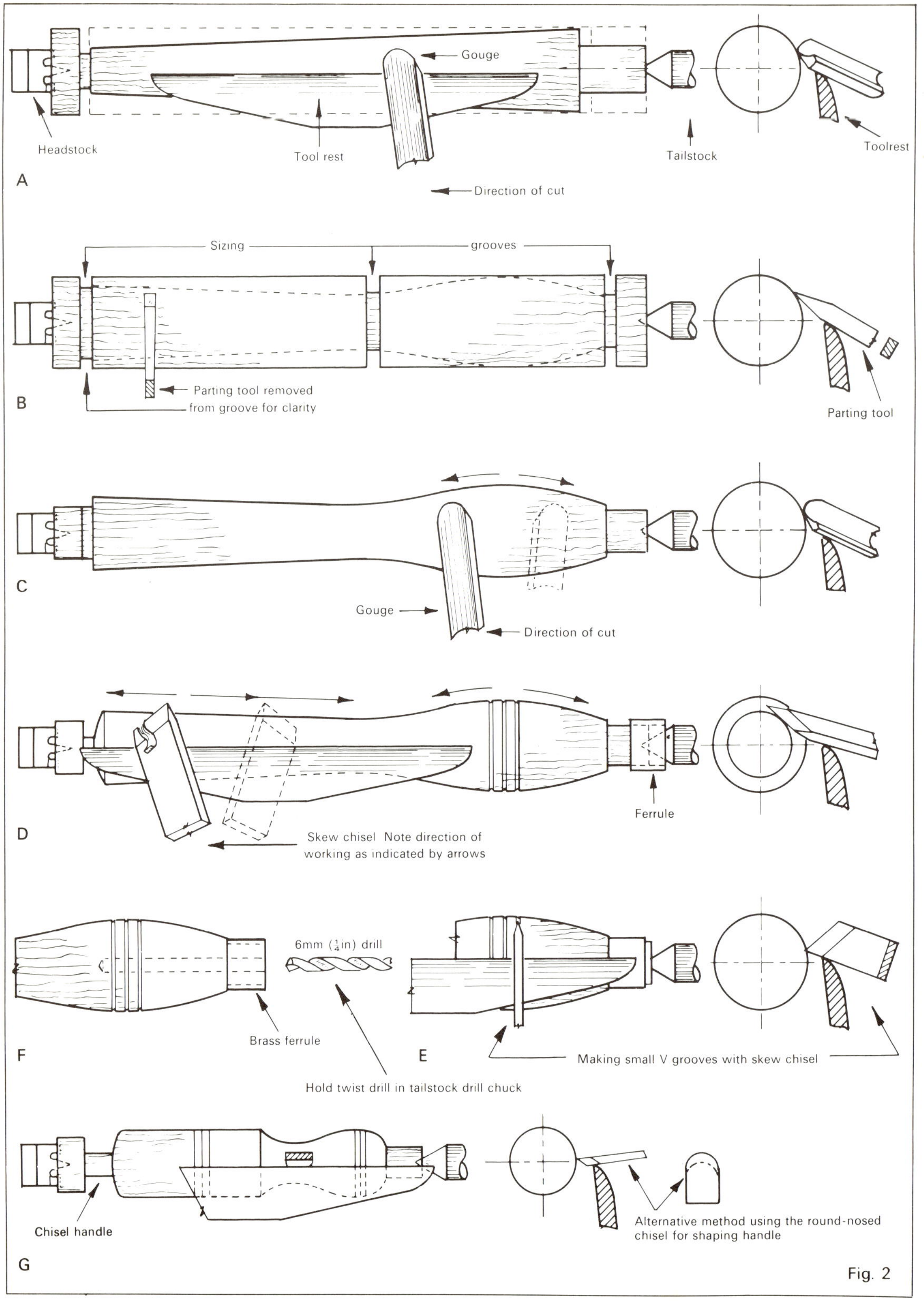
Gouge
Headstock
Tool rest
Tailstock
Toolrest
A
Direction of cut
Sizing
grooves
Parting tool removed
from groove for clarity
B
Parting tool
C
Gouge
Direction of cut
Ferrule
D
Skew chisel Note direction of
working as indicated by arrows
6mm (¼in) drill
Brass ferrule
F
E
Making small V grooves with skew chisel
Hold twist drill in tailstock drill chuck
Chisel handle
Alternative method using the round-nosed
chisel for shaping handle
G
Fig. 2

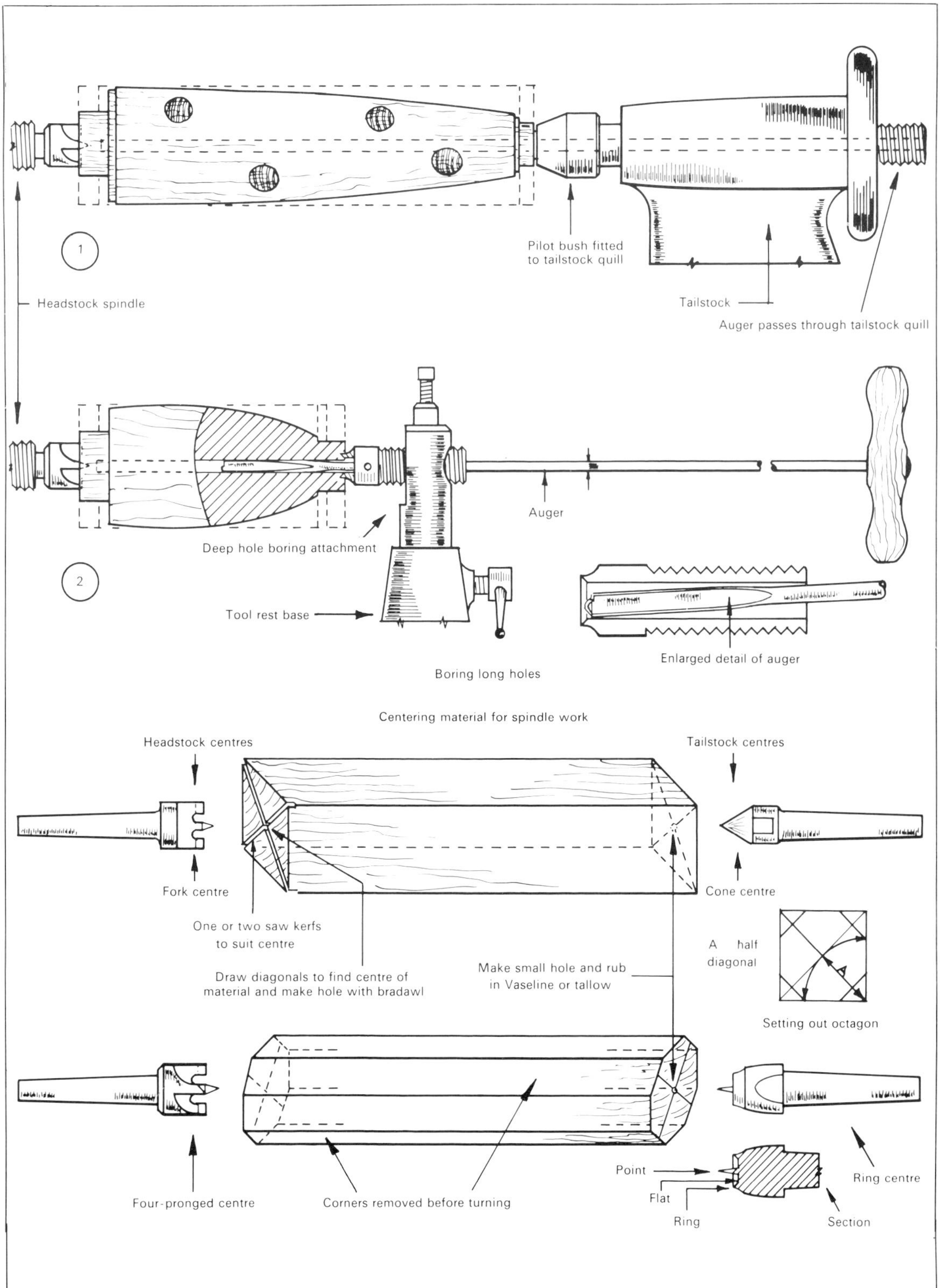
1
Headstock spindle
Pilot bush fitted
to tailstock quill
Tailstock
Auger passes through tailstock quill
2
Auger
Deep hole boring attachment
Tool rest base
Enlarged detail of auger
Boring long holes
Centering material for spindle work
Headstock centres
Tailstock centres
Fork centre
Cone centre
One or two saw kerfs
to suit centre
Draw diagonals to find centre of
material and make hole with bradawl
Make small hole and rub
in Vaseline or tallow
A half
diagonal
A
Setting out octagon
Point
Flat
Ring
Ring centre
Section
Four-pronged centre
Corners removed before turning

Fig. 3

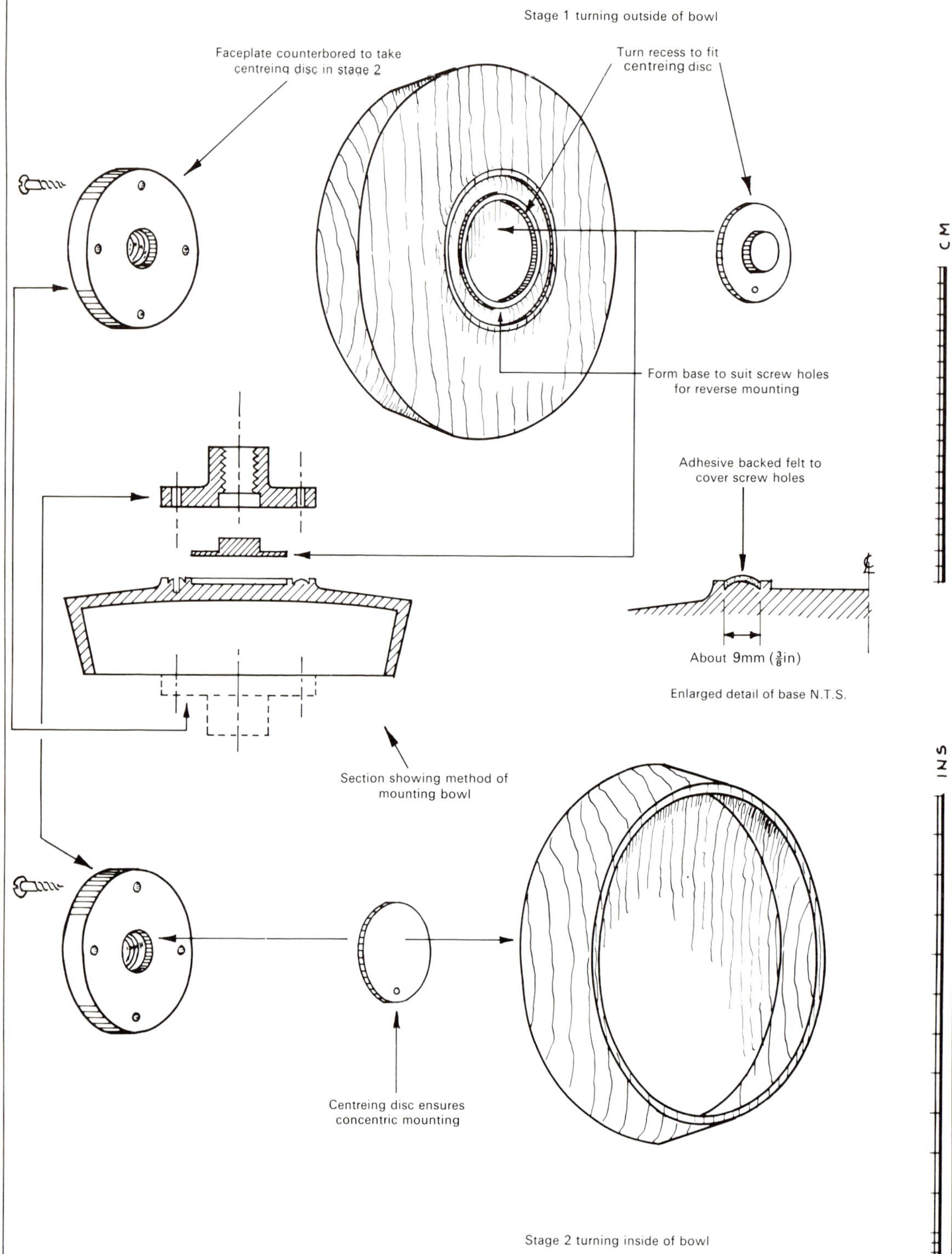
Stage 1 turning outside of bowl
Faceplate counterbored to take centreing disc in stage 2
Turn recess to fit centreing disc
Form base to suit screw holes for reverse mounting
Adhesive backed felt to cover screw holes
About 9mm ($\frac{3}{8}$in)
Enlarged detail of base N.T.S.
Section showing method of mounting bowl
Centreing disc ensures concentric mounting
Stage 2 turning inside of bowl
CM
INS

Fig. 4

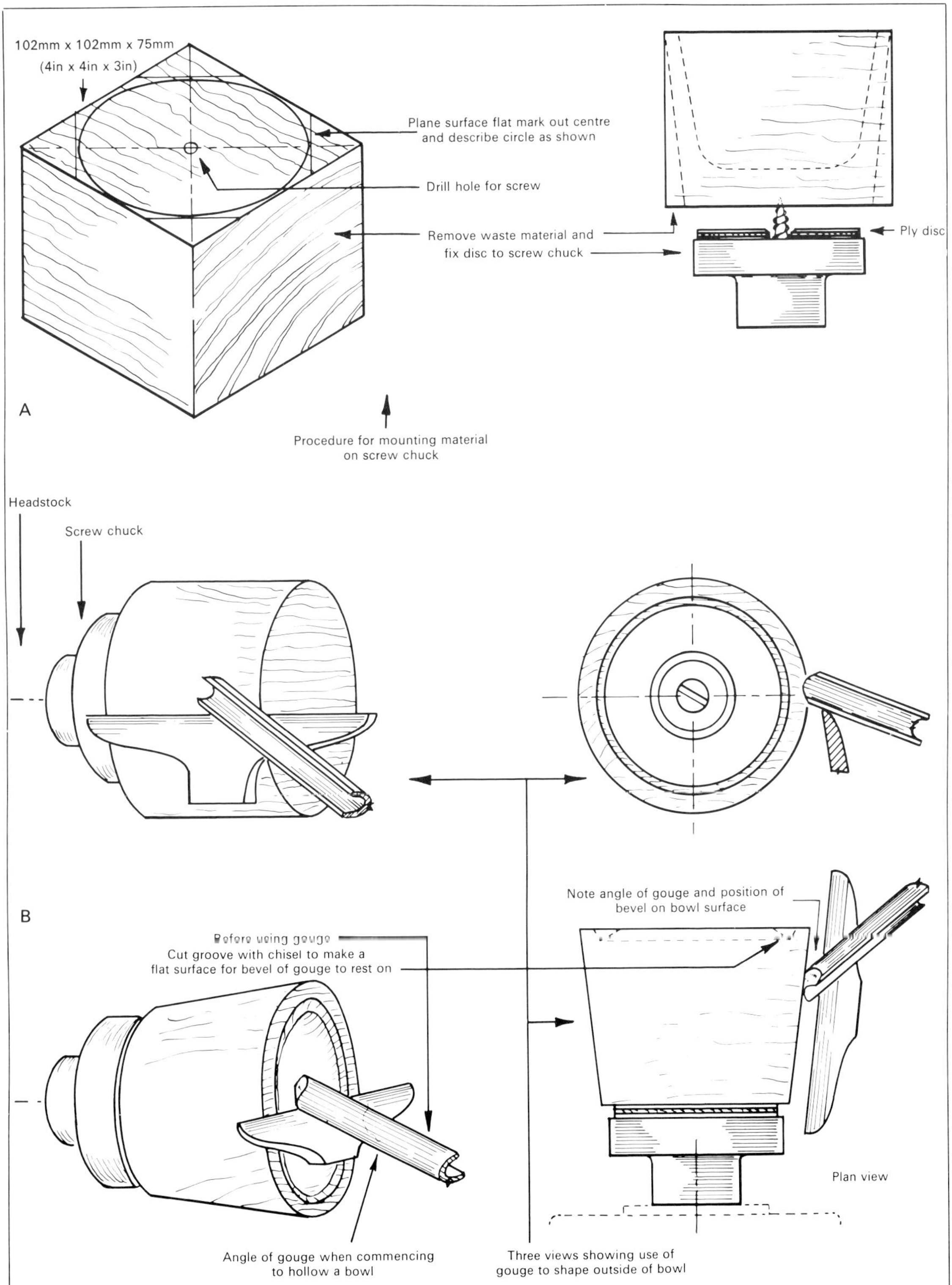
102mm x 102mm x 75mm
(4in x 4in x 3in)
Plane surface flat mark out centre and describe circle as shown
Drill hole for screw
Remove waste material and fix disc to screw chuck
Ply disc
A
Procedure for mounting material on screw chuck
Headstock
Screw chuck
Note angle of gouge and position of bevel on bowl surface
B
Before using gouge
Cut groove with chisel to make a flat surface for bevel of gouge to rest on
Plan view
Angle of gouge when commencing to hollow a bowl
Three views showing use of gouge to shape outside of bowl

Fig. 5

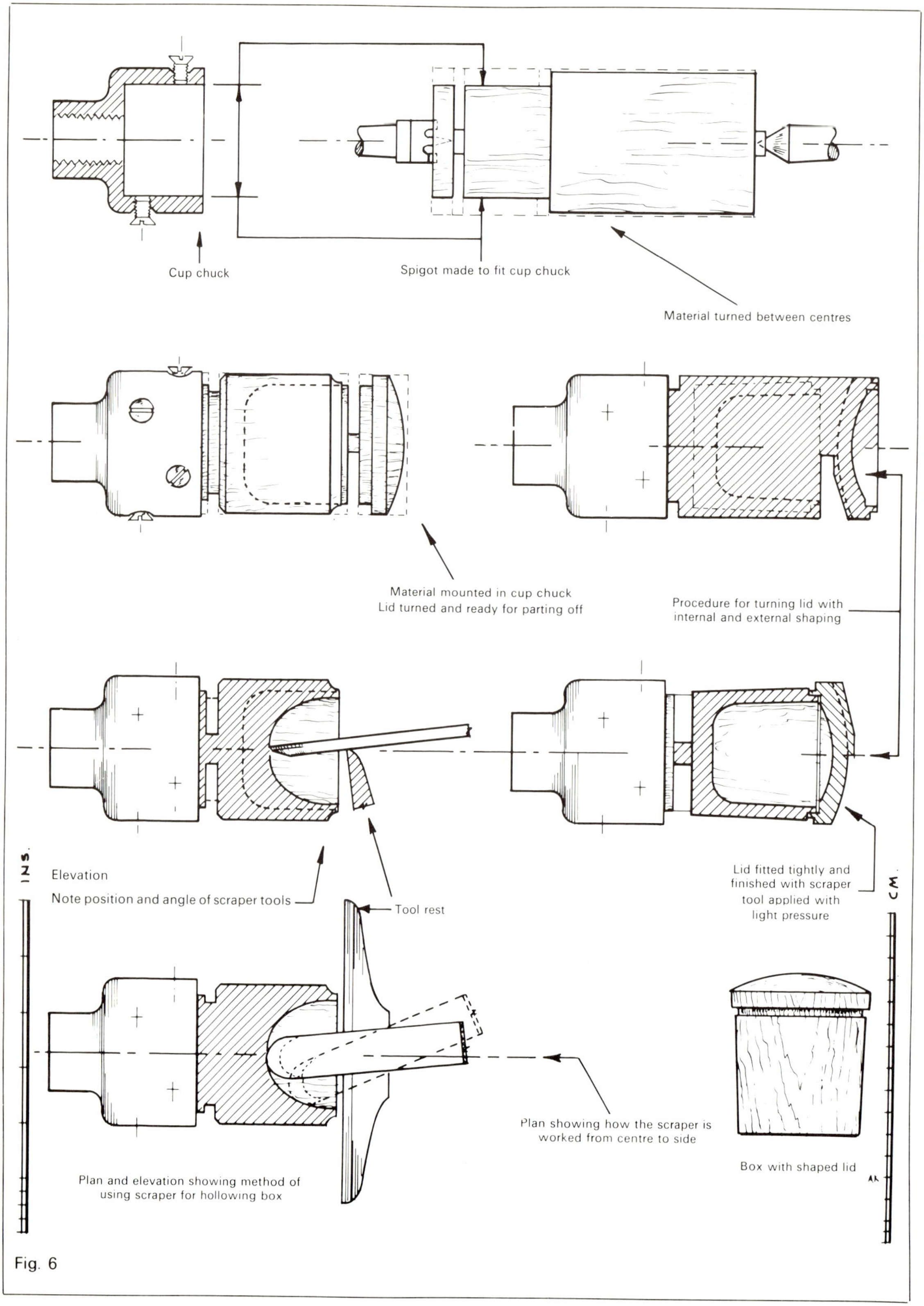

Cup chuck
Spigot made to fit cup chuck
Material turned between centres
Material mounted in cup chuck
Lid turned and ready for parting off
Procedure for turning lid with
internal and external shaping
INS.
Elevation
Note position and angle of scraper tools
Tool rest
Lid fitted tightly and
finished with scraper
tool applied with
light pressure
CM.
Plan showing how the scraper is
worked from centre to side
Box with shaped lid
Plan and elevation showing method of
using scraper for hollowing box

Fig. 6

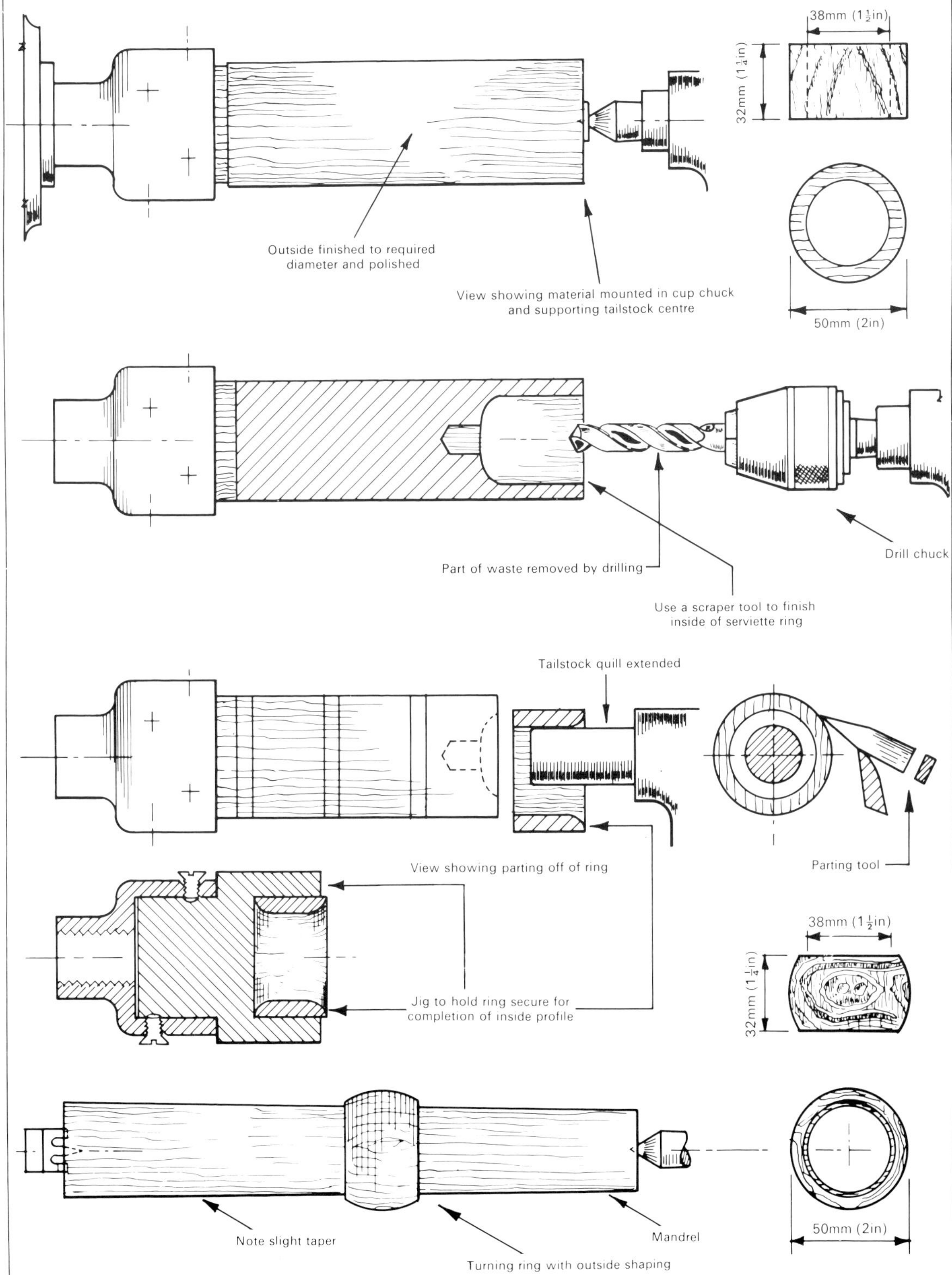
38mm ($1\frac{1}{2}$in)
32mm ($1\frac{1}{4}$in)
Outside finished to required diameter and polished
View showing material mounted in cup chuck and supporting tailstock centre
50mm (2in)
Drill chuck
Part of waste removed by drilling
Use a scraper tool to finish inside of serviette ring
Tailstock quill extended
View showing parting off of ring
Parting tool
38mm ($1\frac{1}{2}$in)
32mm ($1\frac{1}{4}$in)
Jig to hold ring secure for completion of inside profile
Note slight taper
Mandrel
Turning ring with outside shaping
50mm (2in)

Fig. 7

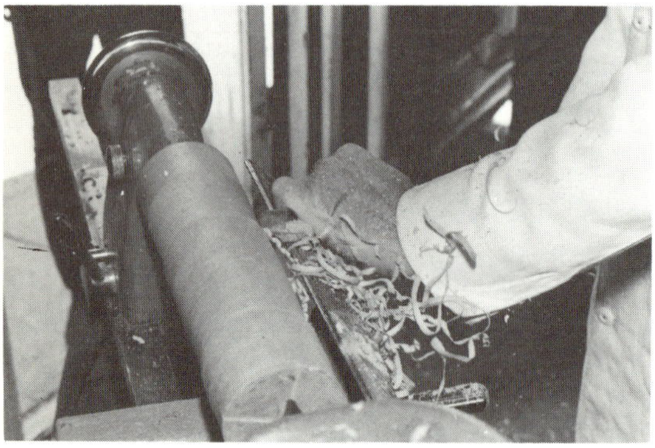

Small bowls make attractive presents and are quite economical to produce. Fig. 5A and B show the methods of mounting the disc on the screw chuck and use of the gouge. These bowls can be turned successfully out of mild working hardwood up to 203mm. (8in.) in diameter. Care must be taken to ensure that the bowl is securely held by the screw. On removing the bowl, the screw hole is plugged and the base covered with baize.

The diagrams in Fig. 6 show the methods of making small, attractive boxes and fitting lids by means of the cup chuck. The latter is a most useful and versatile piece of equipment.

The procedure for making napkin rings is illustrated in the diagrams, Fig. 7. To prevent chattering it is advisable to use short lengths of material not longer than 200mm. ($7\frac{7}{8}$in.) when making boxes and napkin rings.

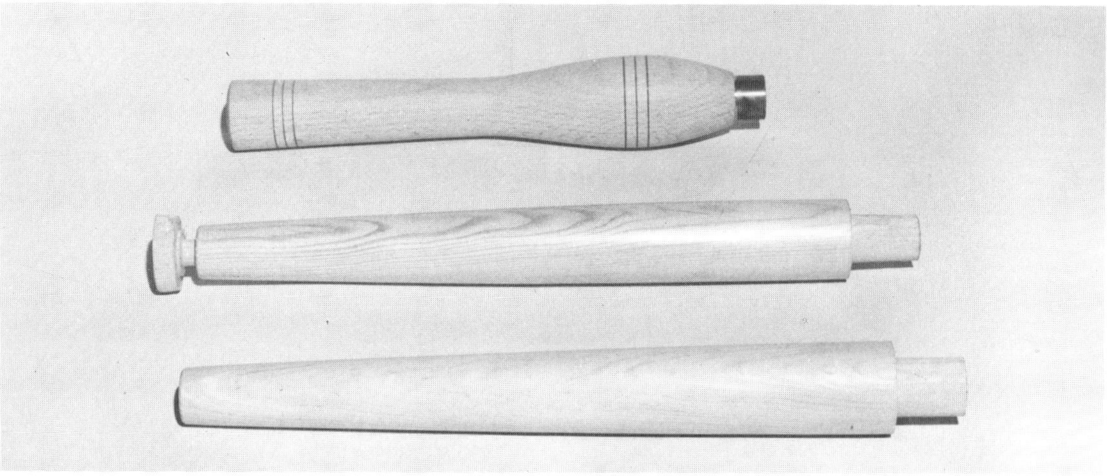

Opposite
Fig. 8 (Left above) Turning between centres using a 38mm ($1\frac{1}{2}$in) rounded-nose gouge.

Fig. 9 (Left below) Second view; note angle of gouge and way in which it is held.

Fig. 10 (Right above) Turning outside of bowl with a 12mm ($\frac{1}{2}$in) deep long and strong gouge. This size of gouge is quite adequate for shaping the outside and inside of large and small bowls.

Fig. 11 (Right below) Turning inside of bowl.

This page
Fig. 12 (Top) Tool handle and table legs. See method of turning, page 106.

Fig. 13 (Below left) Table lamp bases in lime.

Fig. 14 (Below right) Table lamp base in beech.

Fig. 15 (Top) Turned table leg showing technique of jointing rails. The shoulders of the top rail are scribed over the leg while the rail in the foreground is scribed only below the tenon.

Fig. 16 (Centre) Top left shows a faceplate with projecting screw chuck ideal when turning small bowls, 75mm–200mm (3in–about 8in) in diameter. Centre foreground is a drill chuck useful when turning small handles. Below is a small screw chuck with piece of yew attached ready to make a small handle.

Fig. 17 (Bottom) Small bowls 100mm (4in) turned on the screw chuck. The rims are shaped after turning using spokeshaves, rasps, files and sandpaper. The bowls are in teak and acacia.

Fig. 18 (Top right) Bowl in mahogany and laburnum. This blank disc was glued to a soft wood disc with paper between the joint to allow for easy removal, and secured to a 100mm (4in) faceplate for turning.

Fig. 19 (Centre) Group of bowls; left to right in plane, iroko and lime. The latter is reversed to show one method of mounting, see page 108.

Fig. 20 (Bottom) Various small bowls all turned using the screw chuck. Left to right in lime acacia, sycamore and yew.

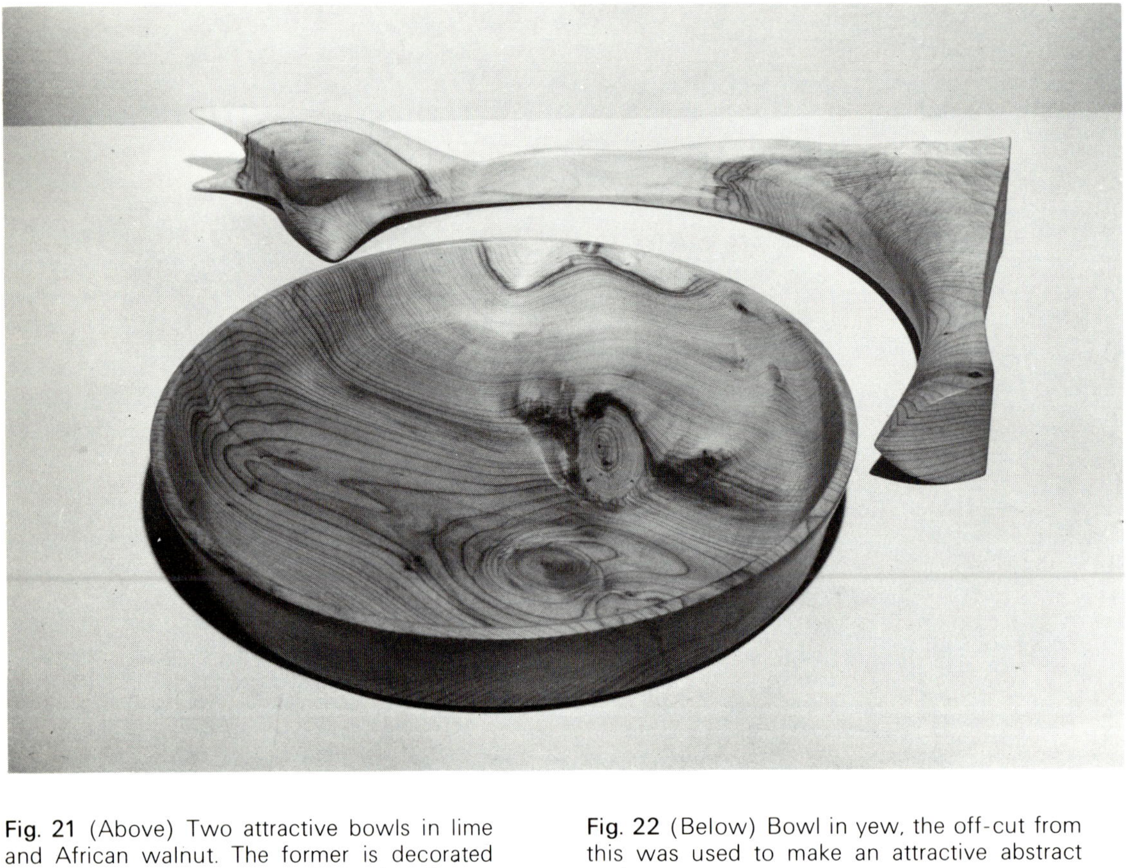

Fig. 21 (Above) Two attractive bowls in lime and African walnut. The former is decorated with burnt-in lines while the other has a sculptured rim.

Fig. 22 (Below) Bowl in yew, the off-cut from this was used to make an attractive abstract sculpture.

Fig. 24

Fig. 23 (Top) Group of napkin rings in sycamore, laburnum, utile and teak. Made from 50mm × 50mm (2in × 2in) material.

Fig. 24 Boxes in teak, 75mm (3in) diameter.

Fig. 25 (Bottom right) Bowl with shaped rim and handles, 254mm (10in) diameter. Made from London plane, the surplus material removed with a coping saw. The rim and handles were finished with spokeshaves, rasps, files and sandpaper.

Fig. 28

Fig. 29

Opposite
Fig. 26 (Top) Boxes in spruce.

Fig. 27 (Centre) Boxes in African walnut. Two boxes have veneered lids, that on the right has a lid of yew. These boxes are all made from 75mm (3in) diameter material.

Fig. 28 Box in African walnut veneered in sycamore and rosewood. The top is slightly convexed.

Fig. 29 Box in sycamore. 75mm (3in) diameter × 100mm (4in)

This page
Fig. 30 (Above) Large bowl fitted with a turntable and set of small bowls, all in lime. Spoons are in laminated rosewood and shaped. Made by a student of Shoreditch College.

Fig. 31 Turned and carved abstract in chestnut. 75mm (3in) diameter × 305mm (12in).

Fig. 31

RED
GOLD
BLACK

Opposite
Fig. 32 (Above) Templates made for offertory plates in oak.

Fig. 33 (Below) Offertory plates for Egham Parish Church. The outline of the shields is incised and the shields are coloured with acrylic paint. 305mm (12in) diameter × 55mm ($2\frac{1}{4}$in).

This page
Fig. 34 (Above left) Stacked offertory plates.

Fig. 35 (Above right) Eggcup stand in muninga and box. Made by a student of Shoreditch College.

FINISHING TECHNIQUES

Wood has an open, cellular structure which, with few exceptions, needs some kind of surface treatment to keep it clean, preserve and protect it from changing atmospheric conditions and to bring out the natural beauty of the grain. A good finish on wood is not possible unless the surface has been properly prepared by planing, scraping and sanding. In some work, as in carving and sculpture, the wood is often left as finished from the tool. *The tooled finish should appear crisp and clean as left from very sharp tools and should not be sanded.*

Preparation
The method of preparing a piece of wood to take a polish is basically the same no matter what kind of polish is used. As an example of general procedure, the method of cleaning up the surface of a piece of hardwood to receive a white French polish or other similar finish is described below.

Sharpen your smoothing plane iron and adjust the cap iron so that it is about 1mm. ($\frac{1}{16}$in.) clear of the cutting edge. Adjust the plane so as to remove a very fine shaving. With a sharp and correctly set plane you should be able to remove a silk-like shaving.

In cases of difficult and interlocking grain which cannot be planed in the direction of the grain without plucking up, it is necessary to finish by planing at right angles or across the grain. This is generally described as traversing. See Fig. 28 showing the profile of a smoothing plane iron, page 32.

A cabinet scraper may be used to remove plane marks or other small blemishes left by the smoothing plane. The material should then be ready for finishing with abrasive paper, or for sanding.

Abrasive paper
Many kinds of paper are available, these include glasspaper (commonly called sandpaper), garnet paper and aluminium oxide paper, which is excellent when used with power sanders. All these papers which usually range from coarse to fine, are graded by numbers or letters.

Sanding
Sandpaper should be used with care. For flat surfaces it should be wrapped round a cork rubber and rubbed in the direction of the grain. Commence with an appropriate grade to suit the work in hand, then continue with consecutively finer grades until the desired finish is produced.

To prevent the initial coat of polish 'raising the grain' the surface should be lightly damped with clean water and allowed to dry before finishing with the finest grade of paper. For high quality work this damping process is often repeated several times before the polish is applied.

French polishing
A well tried and proven finish, and when applied correctly it gives one of the most beautiful and durable finishes. French polish consists of shellac and methylated spirits and can be obtained as, White, Brown, Garnet and Button polish.

Application: French polish is applied with a rubber, consisting of a clean piece of white cotton rag, approximately 300mm. × 300mm. (12in. × 12in.) and a pad of wadding or cotton wool about the size of an egg. The polish should be poured on to the cotton wool until it is saturated.

To make the rubber, place the cotton wool in the centre of the rag and fold into a pear-like shape to fit the hand. The rubber is applied to the work using a circular motion. Several applications may be needed, finally finishing in the direction of the grain.

Brush method of applying French polish: A good quality polisher's mop is essential for the best results. Apply the French polish sparingly with the mop, using two or three thin coats rather than one heavy one. When dry, lightly rub down with a fine grade of sandpaper, or steel wool which has been dipped in wax polish for lubrication. (See notes on wax polishing.) Finish by burnishing with a fairly soft cloth. This process gives a very satisfactory result when used on furniture, sculpture or carvings.
Care of brushes: These should be washed out with methylated spirits and rubbers kept in airtight containers.

Wax polishing
Wax polishing has long been considered one of the best wood finishes, producing a pleasing eggshell gloss. It is suitable for use on furniture and carvings. Generally, a wax finish will not withstand water or heat and should not be used in these situations. The best wax is made from beeswax and pure American turpentine. Beeswax can be easily prepared.
Application: Wax can be applied direct to the prepared wood. The softened wax penetrates the wood surfaces enhancing the figure and adding depth and warmth. Rub the wax well into the wood, leave for approximately 30 minutes and burnish with a cloth. Several applications spread over a few weeks are needed to produce a lustrous finish.

An alternative, and well tried method, which produces quick results is obtained by first sealing the wood with a thin coat of shellac or wood sealer and when dry, lightly sanding it with the finest grade of paper. A pad of fine grade steel wool impregnated with wax can also be used for the initial cutting down. Carefully remove all dust and using a *lint-free* cloth apply the wax evenly over the surface. In some situations a small brush would be advantageous. Leave for approximately 30 minutes and rub vigorously with a clean polishing cloth. Follow with three or four coats of wax over intervals as previously stated.

Note. Steel wool can cause discolouration on some woods—particularly oak—and sandpaper, not steel wool, should be used for rubbing down such woods.

Oil polishing
A mixture of linseed oil and pure American turpentine, when applied to wood—particularly teak, mahogany, walnut, oak, rosewood, elm, laburnum, yew, sapele and cedar—usually produces a fine lustrous surface, enhancing the natural beauty of the wood.

The oil is not applied as a surface coating but is worked into the pores of the wood by hard rubbing. A good lasting and durable finish can be obtained if one is prepared to spend the necessary time.

Application: Apply a mixture of $\frac{2}{3}$ linseed oil and $\frac{1}{3}$ pure American turpentine generously with a cloth and rub well in until the wood has absorbed as much oil as it can take in one application. Using a clean cloth wipe off all surplus oil. The work can now be rubbed vigorously for 10 to 15 minutes with a fairly coarse linen cloth. Repeat this process every seventy-two hours.

It is essential to allow each application to dry before applying the next one. A test for dryness can be made by pressing the thumb on the work for a few minutes; if the surface of the thumb becomes oily it is not dry enough to take another application. The process should be continued until a fine, permanent lustre is obtained. If the oil raises the grain of the wood, when dry, rub smooth with the finest sandpaper.

Olive oil
Kitchen woodware such as salad bowls, servers, cheese boards and platters should

be treated with an occasional wipe over with olive oil.

Polyurethane

For a very hard, heat and scratch resistant finish, Polyurethane may be used. This should be applied strictly in accordance with the manufacturer's instructions.

Painting

Exciting colour contrasts can be produced with paint, when used on masks or other suitable sculptured forms. The work should be primed or sealed before painting and any blemishes made good with a suitable filler. There are many excellent makes of oil and acrylic paints commercially available and it is advisable to read the manufacturer's instructions before use.

Staining

An extensive range of stains is readily available on the market. Some beautiful colour effects can be achieved on softwood and plywood with the use of stains. Make sure the surfaces are finished and free of dust before applying stain. When dry fix stain with shellac or sanding sealer.

Note. Before applying stain to your carving or panels, it is advisable to experiment on a similar piece of wood so that colour, penetration, drying time and the like can be checked.

INDEX